Samuel Hubbard Scudder

The Distribution of Insects in New Hampshire

A chapter from the first volume of the final reportupon the Geology of

New Hampshire

Samuel Hubbard Scudder

The Distribution of Insects in New Hampshire
A chapter from the first volume of the final reportupon the Geology of New Hampshire

ISBN/EAN: 9783337288884

Printed in Europe, USA, Canada, Australia, Japan

Cover: Foto ©Andreas Hilbeck / pixelio.de

More available books at **www.hansebooks.com**

T. e Distribution of Insects in New Hampshire.

A CHAPTER

FIRST VOLUME of the FINAL REPORT

UPON THE

GEOLOGY OF NEW HAMPSHIRE.

BY SAMUEL H. SCUDDER,

CAMBRIDGE. MASS.

CONCORD, N. H.:
EDWARD A. JENKS. STATE PRINTER.
1874.

CHAPTER XII.

THE DISTRIBUTION OF INSECTS IN NEW HAMPSHIRE.

BY SAMUEL H. SCUDDER.

I. GENERAL CONSIDERATIONS.

PROBABLY no state in the Union presents so striking a variety in its animal life as New Hampshire. Its northern and southern portions belong to distinct continental faunas; above the forest growth of its colder region rise some of the highest elevations east of the Rocky Mountains, and these bleak altitudes support a vegetation and an assemblage of animals intimately resembling those of Labrador and Greenland, while sixty miles to the south flourish animals characteristic of subtropical climes.

In the northern hemisphere, rivers flowing south always exert an influence upon the character of the inhabitants upon its banks; and the Connecticut, although navigable but fifty miles, is no exception to the rule. At its southern extremity it reaches a warm coast and a latitude where numerous insects occur, whose true metropolis is found in the Carolinas and Floridas. Many of these, following the course of the river, with its warm, moist banks, penetrate into the heart of the country; some are found in central Massachusetts, a few in southern Vermont and New Hampshire; and one or two are found even in the latitude of the White Mountains. It is therefore especially interesting to consider the distribution of a few groups of insects in New Hampshire.

In 1854, Prof. L. Agassiz made the first attempt[*] to divide North America into several zoölogical areas; and, on a rude map accompanying his sketch, he draws a line in an east-westerly direction, which passes through New Hampshire. The two great regions thus separated he names the Canadian and Alleghanian faunas.

In 1859, Dr. J. L. LeConte divided the United States into a number of "entomological provinces;"[†] and the "northern" and "middle" provinces of his "Atlantic district" were separated by a line which passed through the southern half of New Hampshire.

In 1863, Prof. A. E. Verrill also pointed out that the dividing line of the Canadian and Alleghanian faunas cut New Hampshire in two,[‡] and three years later he defined the limits more exactly as "coincident with a line which shall indicate a mean temperature of 50° Fahrenheit during the months of April, May, and June;" and, in describing its course, says,— "It passes south of Mooschead and Umbagog lakes, but rises somewhat northward along the Androscoggin valley, thence it passes southward of the White Mountains, through the vicinity of Conway, N. H. It bends northward again up the Connecticut valley as far as Craftsbury, Vt., where the mean temperature is 50° 91." [||]

Mr. J. A. Allen has recently discussed the areas of the faunas of eastern North America; and, in his description of the northern boundary of the Alleghanian fauna, says the line "follows the northern boundaries of the lowlands through southern Maine and southern New Hampshire. In the Connecticut valley it rises farther to the northward, and, in its southern descent, skirts the eastern base of the Green Mountains." [§]

Both of these latter writers base their conclusions upon the study of birds during breeding season, as first suggested by Prof. Verrill, in 1866, in the paper from which we have quoted, and where he further writes,—"From this remarkable coincidence between this system of lines of temperature of the months of spring and early summer, with what had been already observed in the actual distribution of birds, we must necessarily infer

---

* Nott and Gliddon: *Types of Mankind*, p. lxxviii, and map.

† *The Coleoptera of Kansas and Eastern New Mexico*. Smiths. Contr. 4to, 1859.

‡ "The Adirondack region of New York, the northern parts of Vermont and New Hampshire, including most of the higher parts of the Green Mountains, and all of the White Mountains, and even the summits of the higher Alleghanies, will be included in the Canadian fauna." *Proc. Ess. Inst.*, iii, 138.

′ *Proc. Bost. Soc. Nat. Hist.*, x, 260.

§ *Bull. Mus. Comp. Zoöl.*, ii, 335 (1871).

that they are chiefly influenced, so far as latitude is concerned, by the
temperature of the breeding season . . . ; whether a similar law con-
trols the distribution of mammalia, reptiles, insects, etc., can only be
determined by further investigation."

Since insects are not regularly migratory animals ; as several genera-
tions frequently succeed each other during a single season ; and, as the
winter is passed in very various conditions, we can hardly expect their
distribution to follow exactly that of birds.   Various causes may modify
unequally the distribution of insects belonging to a certain group: too
intense cold in our arctic winters; the lack of snow during a less severe
season ; too excessive heat or too long a drouth in midsummer; or, too
sudden changes of temperature at critical periods.   Taking our butterflies only, they may be found at every season of the year, even in mid-
winter, of one species or another, in every stage of existence, from the
egg, through all the larval periods and the chrysalis, to the imago.   The
distribution of butterflies is therefore much more complicated than that
of birds, whose early stages are always passed in comparatively warm
weather, under the guardianship of the mother; and, if more than one
brood appears during a season, the second is only the produce of the
same pair that raised the first.

It is nevertheless true that the distribution of insects over continental
areas coincides in a remarkable way with that of birds.   The northern
limits of the Alleghanian fauna, as laid down by Verrill, agree very
fairly with the northern boundary of the belt colored blue on Plate B;
and this probably indicates pretty accurately the southern limit of *Cyclopides Mandan* and the northern limit of *Megisto Eurytus, Grapta comma,
Argynnis Cybele, A. Aphrodite*, and *Euphyes Metacomet*.   It may be ques-
tioned, however, whether, as far as butterflies are concerned, this can really
be considered the northern limit of the Alleghanian fauna.   If we trace
upon a map of the state the northern limits of the several Alleghanian
butterflies and the southern limits of the Canadian, they will be found to
mingle in a broad belt of country, which includes all the colored portions
of Plate B.   The northernmost Alleghanian and southernmost Canadian
species gradually decrease in numbers away from their metropolis, and
become confined to increasingly lower or higher altitudes in this belt,
according as they are Alleghanian or Canadian forms.

Mr. Allen's location of the dividing line between the Alleghanian and Canadian faunas, though rather vaguely stated, seems to correspond better with the distribution of butterflies, though it is perhaps still too far north; and I have colored a narrow band red on Plate B, which will indicate more exactly the limitation which seems to accord best with the facts at my command. This band, striking the Maine boundary opposite the lower extremity of Lake Winnipiseogee, runs in a south-westerly direction nearly parallel with the coast line of Maine, until it reaches the vicinity of the Monadnock mountain (Hillsborough county), and then turns sharply upward and strikes the Connecticut river at the highlands about Claremont. In the neighborhood of this band (sometimes closely confined to it) are the southern limits of such Canadian butterflies as *Minois Alope*, and the northern limits of such Alleghanian butterflies as *Basilarchia Astyanax, Grapta interrogationis, Vanessa Huntera, Speyeria Idalia, Pterourus Troilus, Erynnis Juvenalis, Anthomaster Leonardus,* and *Limochores Manataaqua;* other species, including northern types like *Grapta Faunus* and *Argynnis Atlantis,* and southern types, such as *Epargyreus Tityrus* and *Pamphila Sassacus,* find their southern or northern limits, as the case may be, within other portions of the broad blue belt; while, again, some Alleghanian species, such as *Achalarus Lycidas; Pholisora Catullus, Amblyscirtes vialis, Ocytes Metea,* and *Poanes Massasoit,* find their northern limit at the southern boundary of this belt; and some Canadian species, such as *Argus Eurydice* and *Aglais Milberti,* find at this same point their southern limit.

It is plain that somewhere within this blue belt the dividing line between the Canadian and Alleghanian faunas must be drawn; and it will probably prove difficult to discover any more exact boundary than this, for we should certainly expect an interdigitation of forms peculiar to the two faunas over some common area; and it is only by direct study of the comparative abundance or rarity of very many species of animals within this broad belt that any more exact limitation can be obtained. The local zoölogists of New Hampshire can render science an important service by a careful record of such facts in as many distinct localities as possible; only it is essential that such observations be continued through several successive seasons (best, for a decade), for the comparative abundance of any one species, in any one locality, depends upon a variable

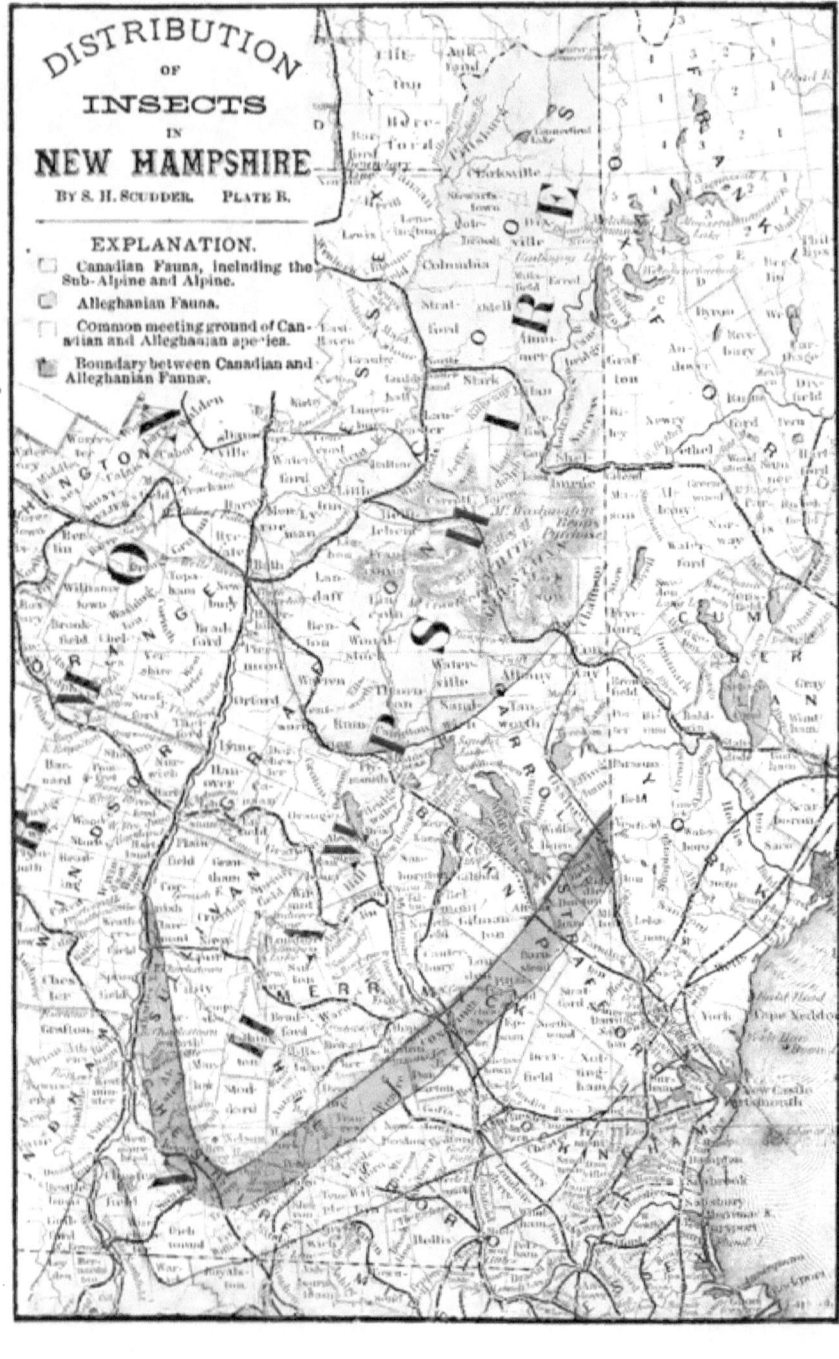

DISTRIBUTION
OF
INSECTS
IN
NEW HAMPSHIRE

BY S. H. SCUDDER.   PLATE B.

EXPLANATION.

☐ Canadian Fauna, including the
  Sub-Alpine and Alpine.

☐ Alleghanian Fauna.

☐ Common meeting ground of Canadian and Alleghanian species.

▨ Boundary between Canadian and
  Alleghanian Fauna.

climate, the antagonism of other insects, and many other causes still unknown.

It may be well to enter with more detail upon the probable limits of the belt colored blue on Plate B. At the north, it enters New Hampshire from Maine near the range of hills lying east of Pinkham's notch, and comes from the direction of Bethel or Norway, Me. That the latter town lies near the boundary between the Alleghanian and Canadian faunas is evident from the extensive collections of Messrs. Verrill and Smith. From this point it runs between Bartlett and Conway toward Plymouth, passing just north of the latter town, following up Baker's river toward the Connecticut, and only crossing the latter stream at some distance above Wells river. At the north, on either side of the White Mountains, the Alleghanian fauna extends along the river bottoms of the Androscoggin, the Connecticut, and even the Ammonoosuc, but too narrowly to be traced upon our map. Less is known about the southern boundary of the band at its eastern extremity, but it must enter the state between Dover and the sea, and it continues in a nearly straight line through Milford to Warwick, Mass. Here it turns upward and toward the Connecticut, crossing the river certainly above Brattleborough, Vt., and perhaps as high as Walpole, N. H., where Mr. S. I. Smith has even taken a specimen of *Laertias Philenor*.

Thus far our examples have been wholly drawn from among the butterflies, as the best known group of insects; but our knowledge of the Orthoptera is sufficiently advanced to show that the facts of their distribution do not militate against the conclusions drawn from the study of the butterflies. Among the Orthoptera of the Alleghanian fauna, *Gryllotalpa borealis*, *Œcanthus niveus*, *Phylloptera oblongifolia*, *Thyreonotus dorsalis*, *Chrysochraon viridis*, and *Diapheromera femorata* appear to reach only the southern limits of our blue belt; while *Tragocephala sordida*, *Œdipoda carolina*, *Hippiscus phœnicopterus*, *H. rugosa*, the different Tettigideans (perhaps with the exception of *Batrachidea cristata*) and *Labia minuta* probably extend to its northern boundaries. On the other hand, among the insects of the Canadian fauna, *Chloealtis conspersa*, *Arcyptera lineata*, *A. gracilis*, *Trimerotropis verruculata*, and *Camnula pellucida* find their southern limit at or near the southern extremity of the blue belt; the latter species also occurs on high ground farther south.

Pezotettix borealis and *P. manca* do not extend below the uppermost boundaries of the blue belt; while, among Alleghanian species, *Trimerotropis æqualis*, *Arphia xanthoptera*, and *A. sulphurea* are limited on the north by the red band, the first perhaps extending somewhat farther.

But the principal interest attaching to the distribution of insects in New Hampshire is through their relation to the White Mountains. These mountains are situated next the southern boundary of the Canadian fauna, and their valleys, as well as the lower wooded portions of their slopes, are peopled with representatives of this region; but their peaks rise from above the limit of forest growth, and maintain a fauna and flora very distinct from those below.

It has long been known that in ascending lofty mountains within the warm or temperate regions, one passes successively over areas exhibiting in their vegetation distinct features, with an ever increasing resemblance to more northern floras. The European Alps have furnished a field for extensive investigations; and their sides have been mapped into distinct zones, called, on an ascending scale, the mountain, the sub-alpine, and the alpine regions. These regions have been recognized and applied to similar phenomena elsewhere, and are in general use. It has also been noticed that the distribution of animals upon mountain summits corresponds with that of plants.

So far as plants are concerned, no distinctive alpine and sub-alpine regions have yet been recognized in the White Mountains. Dr. Asa Gray, it is true, in his statistics of the flora of the northern United States,[*] gives separate and extended lists of alpine and sub-alpine plants; but the only distinction made between the two is, that the former are found only in "our small alpine region" (in which he includes *all* the treeless summits of the White Mountains), and the latter "occur mainly in our alpine region, but are also found decidedly out of it;" so that the lists do not separate plants of distinct alpine and sub-alpine *zones*. Prof. E. Tuckerman, in a very interesting article upon the vegetation of the White Mountains,[†] says,—"Botanists designate the highest bald district, with

---

[*] *Amer. Journ. Arts and Sc.* [2ᵈ, xxii, 251; xxiii, (2, 6).

[†] *The White Hills*, by T. S. King, p. 232.

the heads of ravines descending from it, as the alpine region, and have sometimes spoken of a small tract intermediate between the two, but still imperfectly characterized, as the sub-alpine region;" and this is the most definite mention of a sub-alpine as distinct from an alpine zone yet made by botanists.

More than ten years ago, however, I pointed out [*] that two distinct zones of life existed above the limits of forest growth in the White Mountains, each of which was characterized by the presence of distinct animals. So little has been added to these observations, that I have incorporated them into the present essay.

One feature of the White Mountain vegetation strikes the most casual observer, viz., the abrupt limit of the forest growth upon these mountain slopes, marking a very natural division into a wooded and a woodless district. An observant eye will detect in the latter a further subdivision into two regions,—a lower, where the dwarfed spruce, struggling upward, conceals the gray rocks by a covering of uniform green, broken only by the land-slips which have scarred the declivities with their lengthened furrows, or, by the steeper faces of precipices, where trees obtain no foothold; and an upper, much more restricted area, where the huge blocks of lichen-covered stone lie piled in inextricable confusion, one upon another, or have their interstices filled with sedges, which, on the more level spots, occasionally form small fields like pasture-land, but full of pit-falls and irregularities.

These three zones (the forest district, the district of the dwarfed spruce, and the rocky district) exhibit in a general way the limits of the mountain, the sub-alpine, and the alpine regions; and also correspond, in the characteristics of their inhabitants, to the Canadian, the Hudsonian, and the sub-arctic or Labradorian faunas. They do not, however, correspond to the divisions indicated by Tuckerman, for the "heads of ravines" and all the surrounding districts belong to the sub-alpine region, while the alpine is confined to the topmost areas of only the very highest peaks.

The separation of the mountain from the sub-alpine region is well marked by the limit of the forest growth, and this is so abrupt that a narrow belt of a few rods is usually all that intervenes between the spruce

---

[*] Bost. Journ. Nat. Hist., vii, 612–621 (1863).

of one, two, or three feet high and trees available for the market. The limit of the trees is not wholly dependent upon the elevation of the slope, but is partly influenced by the ravines, and, to a much greater extent, by the exposure of the mountain side, which causes a variation of from one to two hundred feet in altitude. Upon Mt. Madison and the north-western slope of Mt. Washington, the forest line, according to the measurements of Prof. Guyot, reaches the height of 4150 feet above the sea, and, upon the face of Mt. Clinton, which has a westerly exposure, it attains an elevation of 4250 feet; while, again, at the ledge (the most northerly extremity of the sub-alpine region on Mt. Washington), its limit is reached at about 3900 feet. The alpine region occupies the summits of only the three highest mountains, being limited to from one to two hundred feet of the cones of Mts. Adams and Jefferson, and some seven or eight hundred feet of Mt. Washington.

On Plate C I have attempted to show by the red color the general area of the alpine, and by the blue the limits of the sub-alpine region. Standing upon the summit of Mt. Washington, the main peak, and looking at the mountains which lie to the north, it will be seen that, while the sub-alpine region follows the main chain, it extends, also, a short distance along the ridge running eastwardly from the peak of Mt. Madison, and to a much greater distance north-eastwardly from Mt. Washington, in the general direction of the carriage-road, terminating, at a lower level than usual, at the ledge, around which the road abruptly turns just before it enters the forest. South of Mt. Washington there are two ridges: the more prominent and longer range, whose peaks bear the names of American statesmen, trends toward the south-west; the other continues in the direction of the main chain lying to the north of Mt. Washington, and its northernmost peaks have received the names of Davis's and Boott's spurs. A slight abutment to Mt. Washington divides the angle between these two, but is nearer the latter. By the union of these ridges, at their junction with Mt. Washington, there is formed a broad plateau, called Bigelow's lawn, sloping gradually away to the south, where the sub-alpine region finds its widest boundaries, and whose southern limits I have not traced as carefully as upon the opposite side of Mt. Washington, but which must have, approximately, the extent shown upon the map. Within this sub-alpine region, which includes also the heads of all the deeper ravines,

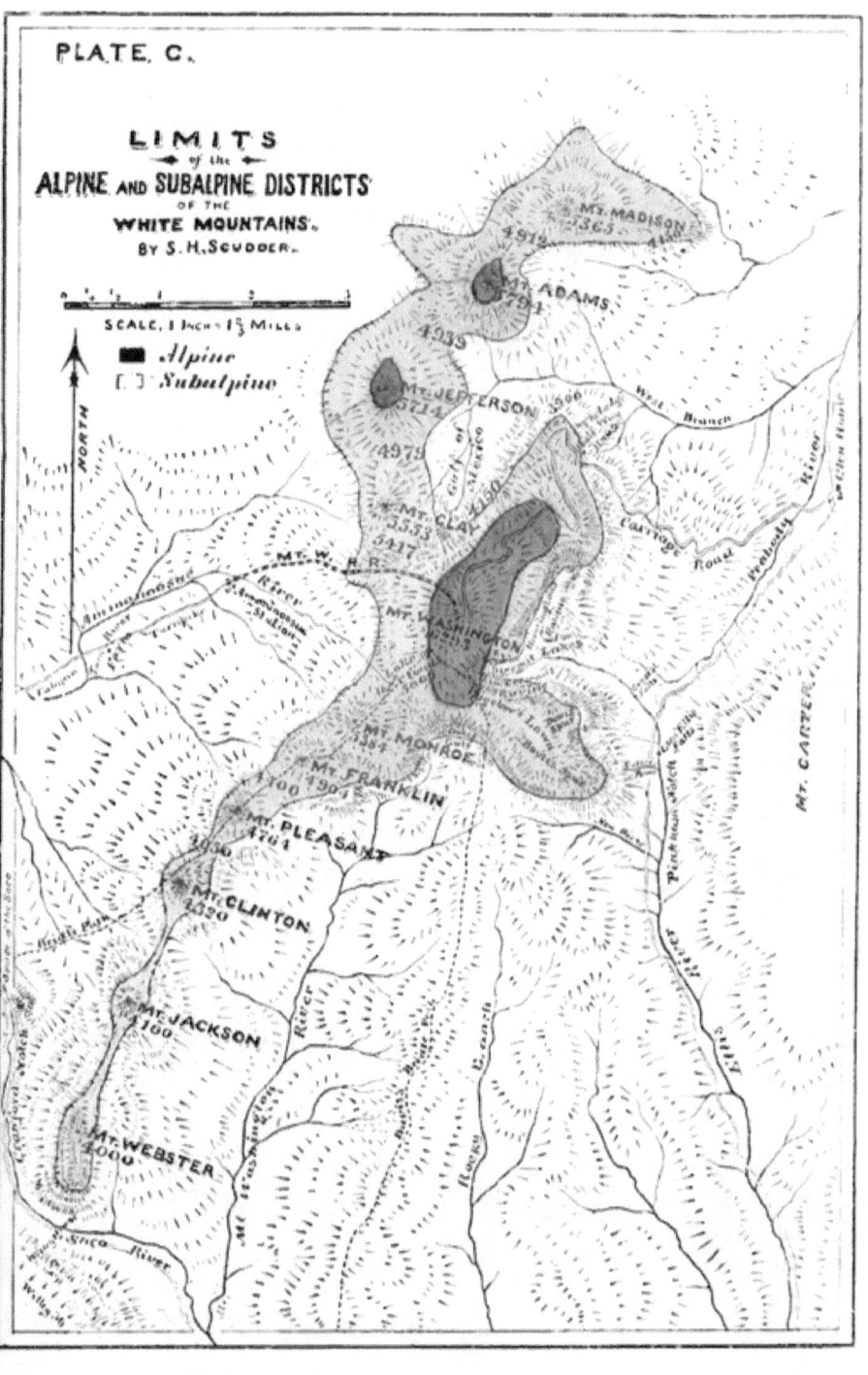

PLATE. C.

LIMITS
of the
ALPINE AND SUBALPINE DISTRICTS
OF THE
WHITE MOUNTAINS,
BY S. H. SCUDDER.

SCALE, 1 INCH = 1⅔ MILES.

■ *Alpine*
[ ] *Subalpine*

there are several ponds or tarns of small extent,—one in the deep gap between Adams and Madison, at the head of King's ravine, at the height of 4912 feet; several small ones upon the slopes of Adams and Jefferson; two deeper ones, known as the Lakes of the Clouds, the highest sources of the Ammonoosuc, lying at the base of Mt. Monroe on the Mt. Washington side; and other small ones on the south side of Mt. Monroe.

The alpine zone of Adams and Jefferson merely encircles their summits; that of Mt. Washington stretches north-eastwardly along the ridge which extends in that direction, occupying one or two successively lower plateaus; it also expands upon the opposite side of the mountain, over the upper portions of the widely extended plateau known as Bigelow's lawn, but it scarcely attains the Lakes of the Clouds upon the one side, or the edge of Tuckerman's ravine upon the other.

Within the limits of the sub-alpine region, and generally preferring its lower to its upper levels, we find a butterfly *(Brenthis Montinus)* and a grasshopper *(Pezotettix glacialis)*, which, so far as yet known, are wholly or almost wholly peculiar to this region. The butterfly has been taken in scanty numbers but at various localities, such as the summit of Mt. Madison, the plateaus just above the ledge, the gaps between Clay, Jefferson, and Adams, the head of Tuckerman's ravine, the adjoining portions of Bigelow's lawn, and the further extremity of the sub-alpine belt upon the summits of Mts. Clinton and Pleasant; it has also been "seen" on the top of Black mountain in Thornton, but some other species of Brenthis might easily have been mistaken for this; yet it will probably be found upon the summits of moderately high and barren mountains in the neighborhood of the White Hills. The grasshopper is abundant upon all the woodless parts of Mt. Madison, especially near the forest line; also, at and above the ledge, near the snow-bank in Tuckerman's ravine, and on the warm hillsides above the latter. It has also been taken on barren hill-tops near Norway, Me., and will doubtless be found in any similar situation in the vicinity of the White Mountain range, especially to the north.

The butterfly belongs to a genus which consists of several groups, some of which are found in the northern temperate regions of Europe and America, extending also into the colder regions. Others inhabit subarctic regions and high altitudes; while one group extends from the sub-arctic into the arctic zone, and contains one representative, which is the most northern butterfly known, *B. polaris*.* Our White Mountain butterfly belongs to the second category, having its representatives on this continent in the Hudsonian fauna. It is very closely allied to two Hudsonian species *(B. Boisduvalii* and *B. Chariclea)*, and at first sight might be taken for them, especially for the former; but repeated examinations of many individuals have confirmed my first impression that they were distinct. The genus Pezotettix, to which the grasshopper belongs, is not so strictly northern as Brenthis, but has several representatives at least in the Hudsonian fauna, and, like Brenthis, is also found in the alpine elevations of Europe.

But even the narrow limit of the alpine zone of the White Mountains claims for its own a single butterfly, which probably has a more restricted range than any other in the world. One may search the season through over the comparatively vast and almost equally barren elevations within the sub-alpine district of the White Mountains, and fail to discover more than here and there a solitary individual whirled by fierce blasts down the mountain slopes, while, a few hundred feet above, the butterflies swarm in great numbers. Every passage of the sun from behind a cloud brings them out in scores, and they may often be captured as fast as they can be properly secured. The contrast between the occasional and unwilling visitor in the sub-alpine region, and the swarms which flutter about the upper plateaus, is most significant. Yet the Carices, the food-plant of the caterpillar, are quite as abundant in the lower regions as in the upper, even to the species *C. rigida*, upon which I found the larva feeding. Now this butterfly, *Œneis semidea*, belongs to a genus which is peculiar to alpine and arctic regions; in fact, it is the only genus of butterflies which is exclusively confined to them. It has numerous members, both in this country and in the old world. One is confined to the Alps of Europe; most of the European species, however, are found only in the extreme north. The genus extends across the whole continent of America, and several of its species occur on the highest elevations of the Rocky Mountains. Several species are common to Europe and America; and it is to one of these that *Œ. semidea* is most closely allied. A few species descend into the Hudsonian fauna; but, as a whole, the genus has its

* This was taken by the Polaris expedition at Polaris bay, their extreme northern station, lat. 82° 16′ N

metropolis farther north.   So that in ascending Mt. Washington, we pass, as it were, from New Hampshire to northern Labrador; on leaving the forests, we come first upon animals recalling those of the northern shores of the Gulf of St. Lawrence and the coast of Labrador opposite Newfoundland; and when we have attained the summit, we find insects which represent the fauna of Atlantic Labrador and the southern extremity of Greenland.*

We have hitherto spoken only of the barren elevations; below these we find the mountain or wooded region corresponding altogether with the Canadian fauna.   The boundary line between this and the Alleghanian fauna crosses the country at about this latitude, and therefore this region forms a promontory of the Canadian fauna stretching southwardly into the Alleghanian fauna, just as occurs to a greater extent along the chain of the Green Mountains, while the Alleghanian fauna, in its turn, extends northward into the Canadian fauna, along the warmer banks of those rivers which find a southern outlet.   We need only wander eight miles north of Mt. Washington itself to find, in the valley of the Androscoggin, the entomological fauna of the central portions of the New England states, while between the two, in the mountain region and in that portion of the Canadian fauna lying in the valley of the Peabody, we have such phenomena as the replacement of *Polygonia comma* of the Alleghanian fauna by *P. Faunus* of the Canadian, and of *Argynnis Aphrodite* by *A. Atlantis.*

We have, then, three distinct faunas upon the slopes of the White Mountains,† each with its characteristic forms.   However much we may expect some difference between the animals of the barren summits and those of the sheltered valleys, we are struck at finding such distinct regions, each sheltering its own peculiar forms, which live, as it were, within a stone's throw of each other, and would seem to be capable of

---

* Dr. A. S. Packard, writing of the region about Hopedale, Labrador, says that he found the species of Œneis in great abundance on the outer barren exposed islands, while those of Brenthis were confined to the valleys of the main land or the southerly slopes of the more protected islands, near the low stunted spruces and the more luxuriant vegetation of that desolate coast.

† It must not be supposed that all the insects which *characterize* the faunas of the barren regions have been mentioned.   I have only chosen a few from many which might be given.   Nearly every year fresh instances are recorded and partial lists have been made.   It is unfortunate, however, that we seldom find any specification of the exact locality or height at which an insect has been taken, or of its comparative abundance; so that the notes at hand are worthless for any purposes of distinction between an alpine and a subalpine fauna; they serve only to show how strikingly the *general* fauna agrees with that of the *whole* of Labrador.

interchanging their stations, and yet which never pass their imperceptible barriers. Many butterflies from the valley occasionally struggle to the extremest summits, and one or two, such as *Polygonia Faunus* and *Aglais Milberti*, are frequently found within the sub-alpine region. In all, the capabilities of flight are unlimited, yet I have but two or three times taken *Œneis semidea* more than a mile and a quarter from the summit; and the appearance of the valley butterflies upon the heights may easily be accounted for, from the fact that all insects with reasonable powers of flight seem to delight in seeking the most elevated situations. Their scanty numbers in these parts is in marked contrast with their often astonishing profusion in their proper haunts below.

The results we have reached, by our study of the faunas of these mountain slopes, are what might be expected from a comparison of the elevation of these mountains with that of the European Alps, at the same time taking into consideration the difference in climate between the two countries. In the Alps the lower limit of the sub-alpine zone is placed by different writers at from 4000 to 4500 feet above the sea, and that of the alpine zone at from 6000 to 6500 feet. Now, although Mt. Blanc lies in a latitude (45° 45′) north of Mt. Washington (44° 15′) by a degree and a half, yet a comparison of the isothermal and isochimenal lines, which pass respectively through these two points, would show that a mountain elevation in Europe, which should have climatic conditions similar to those of the White Mountains, ought to be placed north of the Alps, and would be found between the mountains of Switzerland and Norway at just such a proportionate distance from them as the heights of the alpine and sub-alpine zones of the White Mountains were found to be related respectively to those of the Alps and Scandinavian mountains. By the same comparison we may also judge, that if the summit of Mt. Washington were somewhat less than two thousand feet higher, it would reach the upper limits of the alpine district, or the region of perpetual snow.

An attempt to institute a rigid comparison between the alpine and sub-alpine regions of our White Mountains and those of the Alps is not so easy as would be imagined. If we examine their physical features alone, we shall discover important differences. In New Hampshire these regions are confined solely to the summits of the very highest moun-

tains, all comprised within a few square miles, exposed almost continu-
ously to the very fiercest gales; they are covered by interminable broken
rock-masses, concealed in part by a scanty layer of mould, supporting
either sedges, or stunted juniper-like spruces, whose gnarled and spreading
branches creep along the ground. In Switzerland and the Tyrol these
regions extend over an area of thousands of square miles, more or less
continuous; the highest mountains rise above them into the region of
perpetual snow, and form barriers to the wind, rendering the alpine slopes
scarcely more breezy than the plains. About the Belalp, above Brieg,
where I have paid most attention to the insects of the high Alps, the
trees seem to reach a general level of about 6000 feet;[*] above them the
ground is sward, richly beautified by flowers, and a pasturing ground
for goats and cattle; on the slopes most exposed to the morning and
midday sun, immense patches of low, dark green shrubbery, seldom
rising more than a foot above the ground, dispute the soil with the grass.
These patches consist mainly of heather (Calluna) with Rhododendron and
several species of Vaccinium, and seem to represent the dwarfed spruces
of our alpine heights, which, near the forests, are also accompanied by
Vaccinium. The sward extends up to the snow and cliffs, and while
sedges are no doubt present, its mass is composed of Gramineæ.
During the few days early in July spent in this region, I noticed that
insects, especially butterflies, were most numerous between 5500 and
8000 feet above the sea. The most abundant species of the very highest
region were *Pieris Callidice* and *Erebia Manto;* and many caterpillars of
Melitæa Cynthia were found, crawling about the rocks. Between 6500
and 7500 feet, the more common species were *Syrichtus malvæ, Œneis
Aello* (not rare), *Brenthis Pales* (common), two or three species of
Erebia, including *E. Manto, Colias Palæno* (common), and *Pieris Callidice* (common); *Vanessa Atalanta* and *Aglais urticæ* were also seen, the
latter frequently; the species of Œneis and Brenthis seemed to occupy
an identical zone. Lower down, the Blues appeared in abundance, with
different species of Erebia; *Parnassius Apollo* occurred in considerable
numbers, *Syrichtus malvæ* was extremely abundant, *Aglais urticæ* was
very common, and eggs and young caterpillars could be found anywhere;

---

[*] Though the mountain slopes are often covered with large tracts of pasture land far below this,—a phenom-
enon unknown in the White Mountains.

even *Œneis Aello* was not infrequent, but *Pieris Callidice* was not seen.

Œneis Aello was very wary, and possessed of a very vigorous, energetic flight; *Œ. semidea*, on the other hand, has a very weak flight, and suffers itself to be blown about at random by the wind. This difference seems all the more striking when we remember that *Œ. semidea* inhabits a region of tempestuous winds, where existence would seem impossible to a butterfly, unless unusually gifted. Both species, when at rest, sit with wings back to back, the front pair concealed as much as possible between the hind pair; but *Œ. Aello* always sits erect, or only slightly inclined, while *Œ. semidea* is rarely erect, and often, when it has alighted upon the horizontal surface of a rock or by the muddy brim of a pool, fairly lies upon its side, as if dead.

In the following pages we give a list of the butterflies and Orthoptera of New Hampshire, as far as they are known. The list of Orthoptera is given almost entirely from memoranda collected by myself. For notes on the butterflies, I am indebted to many persons, but especially to Mr. C. P. Whitney, of Milford, N. H. In this list I have incorporated as full an account as possible of the two butterflies peculiar to the barren summits of the White Mountains.

II. List of the Butterflies of New Hampshire, with Notes on their Geographical Distribution.

The names used in the accompanying list are those of my Systematic Revision of some of the American Butterflies.

NYMPHALES.

1. *Œneis semidea* Butl.

[Plate A, Figs. 2, 4, 6, 9, 11, 13, 14: 2, imago; 4, chrysalis, dorsal view; 6, ib., side view; 9, larva, dorsal view of hinder extremity; 11, ib., head; 13, ib., side view; 14, ib., dorsal view.]

As stated in the first part of this memoir, this insect probably occupies a more restricted geographical area than any other butterfly in the world, the narrow area of the alpine fauna of the White Mountains. Dr. Harris's assertion that "it has also been seen on the Monadnock mountain, and will probably be discovered on the tops of the high mountains in our own state" (Massachusetts), is wholly erroneous. I have ascended Grey-lock, the highest mountain in Massachusetts, more than twenty times, and at all seasons of the year, and certainly could not have failed to see this butterfly did it occur there. Since Monadnock is a naked peak, it would certainly be a more propable habitat for the insect; but the limita-tion of its distribution in the White Mountains wholly forbids the possi-bility of its presence on a much lower and isolated mountain to the south.

The butterfly is found most abundantly from about one quarter to three quarters of a mile from the summit of Mt. Washington, or at an elevation of from 5600 to 6200 feet above the sea. It often alights on the flowers of *Silene acaulis* Linn., and also upon some of the Ericaceæ, particularly on a species of Vaccinium; but the best collecting places are the sedgy plateaus of the north-eastern and southern sides of the mountain, where the collector will also obtain a good footing, a matter of no small importance on such a collecting ground. I have never found the butterfly at the head of any of the deep ravines.

Dr. Meyer-Dür states of Œ. Aello, the species occurring in the Euro-pean Alps, that it inhabits the calcareous and central mountains,—not the highest chains, as has been generally supposed, but rather the middle regions, from 4000 to 6000 feet above the sea.* He also makes the remarkable assertion that the butterfly appears, at least in Switzerland,† only on *alternate* years, namely, those with even numbers. Prof. Frey thinks this to be true only for each special locality, but that every year it may be found in some of them.

All the species of this family of butterflies, so far as they are known, feed in the caterpillar state on grasses; ‡ but as the true grasses are rare in the inhospitable region where this insect is found, being replaced almost altogether by sedges, the caterpillar feeds upon the latter. Mr. Sanborn has seen them eating it by day, and, by the aid of a lantern, I discovered

---

* See our previous remarks on this species, p. 343.

† Meyer-Dür says further, that the records of its capture out of Switzerland are also in even years; but, since writing the above, I notice that Speyer, in his work on the geographical distribution of the Lepidoptera of Ger-many and Switzerland (II, 271), says that, according to Trapp, it appears every year, but in some years more abundantly than in others.

‡ This is not strictly true, as I thought when writing it. Boisduval, Rambur, and Graslin, in their work on the caterpillars of Europe, state that *Cœnonympha Corinna* feeds both on Triticum and Carex; and Wilde, accord-ing to Kaltenbach (Pflanzenfeinde, 728), gives Lolium and Carex as the food of *Pararge Achine*.

them feeding on the same plant, *Carex rigida*, by night. This shows that I was mistaken in a belief formerly expressed, that they fed upon lichens.

Œneis semidea was first discovered about half a century ago, and described by Say from specimens sent him by Dr. Pickering and Prof. Nuttall, of Boston. Very few specimens seem to have been taken since that time, until 1859, when I made my first considerable collections in the White Mountains. I ascended the highest peak on July 8, for the express purpose of finding the butterfly, and secured my first specimen at about a mile from the summit, near the foot-path from the Glen. On ascending, the butterfly became more abundant; and, although our party hastened over the ground, more than forty good specimens were taken, and a friend even captured seven without a net. Less than a week afterwards, in a little more than an hour's collecting, fifty-nine were taken, for, in its season, this butterfly is exceedingly abundant.

Dr. Harris gives "June and July" as the season of the flight of the imago, the former date on the authority of Oakes, who found the insect abundant in June, 1826. Undoubtedly this was toward the close of the month. It usually begins to appear very early (the first week) in July, becomes exceedingly abundant before the middle of the month, and continues until about the second week in August. Mr. Sanborn gives July 4th as its earliest appearance in 1869, and only one more specimen was seen before the 9th, although the weather was favorable. This may serve, I think, as an average date, and the butterflies will best be taken in the second and third weeks in July. They lay their eggs until about the 22d of July, and probably a little later. These are apparently dropped loosely among the sedges, for I could obtain no eggs on the sedge itself from gravid females confined in open kegs, and finally, searching among the roots as a last resort, I discovered a single egg, which, however, never hatched. Caterpillars have been found by Mr. Sanborn, the late Mr. Shurtleff, and myself, nearly full grown, on the 2d of August, and others certainly full grown on August 19. More recently Mr. Whitney has found them "apparently fully grown, under stones." They were unquestionably seeking a good place to undergo their transformations. They probably transform to chrysalids at once, and hibernate in that state, although it is possible that they winter as Mr. Whitney found them. In the early part of July, 1869, Mr. Sanborn searched very carefully for the chrysalids of this species, spending ten or twelve hours in raising movable surface stones, and in four or five places clearing away to the depth of several feet the smaller blocks of stone lying in the " rock rivulets," as he appropriately terms the slight gulleys wholly devoid of vegetation, which are scattered everywhere over the plateaus, and which mark the course of the surface waters after rain. He succeeded in securing only two living specimens. Nine others were either infested by ichneumons (*Eulophus semideæ* Pack., and *Encyrtus Montinus* Pack., described below*), or were the empty shells of the previous year. They were all found imbedded between the sides of the rock and the long, dense, crisp moss surrounding it, between half an inch and an inch and a half below

---

* "*Eulophus semideæ* nov. sp. [Fig. 46]. Belongs apparently to the same section of the genus as *E. anemptsimus* Walk.

"♂ (two specimens). Antennæ filiform, not increasing in width toward the tip, rather long, much longer than in *E. anemptsimus*, and very hairy, dark brown. Head deep blue, shining, punctured as usual, under a not powerful lens; mandibles, and other mouth parts, pale piceous; thorax, as well as the whole body, deep blue; fore wings broader at end, clear; spur distinct, dilated at tip; coxæ concolorous with body; trochanters and femora brown, tips of latter pale testaceous; tibiæ brown, pale at tip, or almost wholly pale; tarsi dark on terminal joint, the last joints of hinder pair dark; abdomen as long as the thorax, narrow lanceolate oval, subacutely pointed, more so than in *E. anemptsimus*, concolorous with rest of body, but with steel blue reflections at base. Length, .06 inch."

Fig. 46.

"♀ (ten specimens). Eyes rather larger, and a little nearer together than in the ♂ ; antennæ longer in proportion than in *E. anemptsimus*, the club being much longer. The whole body is shorter and broader than in *E. anemptsimus* and *E. enconganus* Walk., the abdomen especially being much broader, and the apex less attenuate; of the same color as the ♂, with the base of the abdomen more distinctly steel blue. Body smooth and shining, not perceptibly punctate under a strong lens. Legs; trochanters whitish at tip; femora dark brown, whitish at each end; tibiæ and tarsi white, the terminal joint of tarsi dusky. Length .08 inch."

"*Encyrtus Montinus* nov. sp. [Fig. 47]. Closely allied to *E. Swederi* of Europe (Walker's type).

"♀ (one specimen). Ocelli placed in a narrow triangle; eyes large and near together; head and body beneath testaceous; a row of minute pits along the orbits in front, rather remote from the eyes; mouth parts concolorous with the head; antennæ; joint two flattened, clavate; joints one to three darker than the head, four to seven brown, eight and nine yellowish, ten and eleven (club) blackish; the eight terminal joints hairy; prothorax concolorous with the head; the rest of the thorax and the propodeum bluish green (not very dark) with metallic reflections; surface smooth and shining, with small, not dense punctures; sides of thorax below the insertion of wings, and legs dark testaceous; tegulæ dull testaceous; wings smoky, paler toward the outer edge, with a broad, curved, conspicuous white band, extending from the pterostigma, where it is dilated, across to the inner edge of the wing; pterostigma with a slight spur toward the centre of the wing, enclosing a narrow V-shaped space; abdomen regularly triangular, the tip acute, a little longer than broad, being being pretty short, dark brown, shining, sending off dull metallic hues; under side of a paler bronze color. Length .09 inch."

Fig. 47.

"Differs from *E. Swederi* in not having any twin tuft of hairs on the mesoscutum, and in the broadly dilated second antennal joint; the middle pair of legs has a large tibial spur, larger than in *E. Swederi*, and the middle tarsi are larger; otherwise, except in the remarkable differences in coloration, it apparently belongs to the same section of the genus as *E. Swederi*."

" ' Found alive in an old chrysalis case of *Œ. semidea*,' Mt. Washington. F. G. Sanborn."—*Communication of Dr. A. S. Packard.*

the general surface, where the caterpillars had entered. They were not attached to the rock or the moss, but lay in horizontal oval cells, evidently formed by the movements of the caterpillar before pupation. The most particular examination revealed no trace of any web or silken thread, even as a lining of the cell. Mr. Sanborn's impressions, drawn mainly from a comparison between the slender number of specimens he obtained and the abundance of the butterfly, are, that the healthier caterpillars penetrate even deeper into the ground; but as I have also found them under or beside surface stones, and Mr. Whitney has discovered larvæ ready for their change in similar localities, I am more disposed to believe that the place to seek them is beneath and beside the uppermost stones, and especially at the edges of the "rock rivulets," where the vegetation is usually the freshest. To one familiar with the locality,—a surface almost completely strewn with angular rock fragments,—Mr. Sanborn's exploration will seem to have been a very successful one. Most of his specimens were found at more than a mile from the summit; doubtless better success would attend efforts in localities not more than half or three quarters of a mile from the top.

One would suppose that insects, whose home is almost always swept by the fiercest blasts, would be provided with powerful wings fitting them for strong and sustained flight; but the contrary is true. They can offer no resistance to the winds, and whenever they ascend more than their accustomed two or three feet above the surface of the ground, or pass the shelter of some projecting ledge of rocks, they are whirled headlong to immense distances, until they can again hug the earth. Their flight is sluggish and heavy, and has less of the dancing movement than one is accustomed to see in the Oreades.[*] They are easily captured.

The European Aello appears, says Meyer-Dür, among the earliest butterflies of the Alps. It is seen soon after the snow melts,—first, on the lower grounds at the end of May; last, on the higher levels (corresponding more nearly to those to which our species is restricted) at about the beginning of July; it disappears in the same way from the end of June to the end of the first week in August.

2. *Enodia Portlandia* Scudd. Within the limits of New England this is a very rare insect. It may be found occasionally upon the banks of

---

[*] See p. 316.

the southern Connecticut, since Mr. Emery reports that it is "not uncommon" in certain stations about Holyoke and Mt. Tom in Massachusetts. I have also taken two battered specimens at Jefferson, in the White Mountains. Gosse took it at Compton, Lower Canada, and D'Urban on the River Rouge, north of the Ottawa; three or four specimens have also been captured at Suncook, N. H. (Thaxter).

3. *Minois Alope* Scudd. This insect is tolerably abundant, sometimes very common, in the southern half of New England, occurring throughout Massachusetts and the two states lying south of it, and in the southern extremities of Maine, New Hampshire, and Vermont. The most northern localities from which I have seen specimens, or received notes of its capture, are Norway, Me. (Smith), Thornton and Shelburne, N. H. (Faxon), and Sudbury, Vt. Mr. Jones states that it is also found in Nova Scotia. It occurs in open woods and orchards, as well as along roadsides and stone walls, especially such as are overgrown with brambles or skirted by shrubbery.

4. *Minois Nephele* Scudd. This insect is found over the whole northern half of New England in great abundance. The only locality in which I have met with it in Massachusetts is the elevated region about Williamstown, but it undoubtedly approaches closely to the northern limits of the state.

5. *Argus Eurydice* Scudd. In New England this is not a very rare insect, especially in the northern and elevated parts. There is no notice of its capture south of Massachusetts, nor in the Connecticut valley south of New Hampshire. In the latitude of the White Mountains, and as far south as Campton, it will be found extremely abundant by those who look for it in its proper haunts, elevated moist meadows.

6. *Megisto Eurytus* Scudd. The northern limit of this butterfly probably follows the isotherm of 45°, for this seems to be its boundary in New England, since it is found in some abundance in Walpole (Smith) and Milford, N. H. (Whitney). There is no record of it farther north, excepting at Norway, Me., where Mr. Smith found it in abundance; at Plymouth, where it is not very common (Scudder); and at Brunswick, Me. (Packard), toward which place, being on the sea-coast, the isotherm probably turns. It does not occur among the White Mountains, but probably will be found close to their southern boundaries, and quite as far north in Vermont.

7. *Danaus Plexippus* Latr. This butterfly ranges over the whole North American continent from Atlantic to Pacific (excluding perhaps the Rocky Mountain district), as far north as the annual isotherm of 40°, and over that portion of South America lying east of the Andes and north of Rio de Janeiro, including, also, many and perhaps all of the West India islands. It occurs throughout New England, but it is much more rare in the northern than in the southern part, though even here it can hardly be called abundant, for, usually, specimens must be captured singly. Yet, now and again, it swarms, as in the autumn of 1871. In some localities it is especially numerous,—such places, for instance, as islands off the coast, or broad sandy sea-beaches, where no Asclepias grows. Is it that an innate propensity for geographical extension leads it to the last possible limit? Mr. L. L. Thaxter states that it is found in great numbers on Appledore, the largest of the Isles of Shoals, which has a surface of about 500 acres; yet there is no trace of milk-weed upon any of these islands, which he has thoroughly explored. It has not been recorded from the White Mountains.

8. *Basilarchia Disippe* Scudd. Within New England, Disippe occurs abundantly in the south, sparingly in the north, although found in the very heart of the White Mountains. Gosse does not record it from Compton, Canada; and the northernmost points from which specimens have been reported are Mt. Desert (Scudder), Waterville (Hamlin), and Norway, Me. (Smith), the Glen, White Mountains, and Sudbury, Vt. (Scudder).

9. *Basilarchia Astyanax* Scudd. The general range of this butterfly is similar to that of the preceding, though less extensive. It is tolerably abundant in the southern parts of New England, and occurs about as far north as the annual isotherm of 45°, the northernmost points recorded being Dublin (Faxon) and Milford, common (Whitney).

10. *Basilarchia Arthemis* Scudd. This species of Basilarchia has a very different range from the two preceding, its southern limits nearly coinciding with the northern boundaries of *B. astyanax*. In New England it has not been taken south of Massachusetts, and but rarely in that state. It is already common at Brattleborough, Vt., Walpole (Smith), Weare (Emery), and Dublin, N. H. (Faxon and Leonard); but it is said to be scarce in Milford (Whitney), and in the immediate neighborhood of

Dublin.   In the White Mountain region, and in northern New England generally, it is exceedingly abundant, far more so than the other species of the genus in their most favorable localities.   Indeed, the matrons of farm-houses, in the valley of Peabody river, complain of the insects entering the kitchens in such numbers as to be a very nuisance.   One of them, Mrs. Dolly Copp, of "Imp cottage" (well known to many frequenters of "the Glen"), relates how she has taken more than fifty on the inside of her windows in a single morning.

11. *Polygonia interrogationis* Scudd.   In New England this butterfly is nowhere very abundant, and in the northern portions very rare.   The northernmost localities from which it is reported are Brunswick (Packard) and Norway, Me. (Smith), and Walpole (Smith) and Milford, N. H., one specimen only (Whitney).

12. *Polygonia comma* Scudd. is found throughout New England, excepting in the White Mountain region, and perhaps other elevated portions of the northern counties.   It has, however, been taken on Camel's Hump, Vt. (Sprague), and given as a probable inhabitant of Norway, Me. (Smith).

13. *Polygonia Faunus* Scudd.   This butterfly is as peculiar to the Canadian fauna as *P. comma* is to the Alleghanian.   In New England it is found only in the north, the southernmost localities from which it has been recorded being Williamstown, Mass. (Scudder), Dover and Camel's Hump, Vt. (Sprague), Dublin (Faxon) and Milford, N. H., two specimens (Whitney), and Norway, Me. (Smith).   In the valleys of the White Mountains it is exceedingly abundant, and is the butterfly oftenest seen in deep ravines and on mountain slopes below the sub-alpine region.   More than any other species belonging to the mountain region, it mounts to the very summit of the highest peaks, far above any plant upon which its larva would be likely to feed.   Edwards reports a single specimen from West Virginia, and Abbott records it from the mountains of Georgia!   I consider *P. gracilis* a dimorphic form of this species.

14. *Polygonia Progne* Hübn. [Plate A., Fig. 12.]   The range of this butterfly corresponds very closely with that of *P. comma*.   In New England it is more generally distributed and universally common than any other species of Polygonia.   It is somewhat more abundant in the southern than in the northern parts.   I have this spring taken a single specimen in the White Mountain region.   It is common in some seasons at

Norway. Me. (Smith), and has been found at Thornton and Shelburne, N. II. (Faxon). It will probably prove to be rare in the elevated regions of northern New Hampshire and Maine.

15. *Nymphalis J. album* Scudd. occurs throughout New England, although very rare in the northernmost portions. In the White Mountain district and its vicinity it is abundant, as it doubtless is through all that portion of New England lying north of the isotherm of 40°, for the spring months. Mr. Roland Thaxter mentions it as exceedingly common at Suncook, but it is much less so at Milford (Whitney).

16. *Papilio Antiopa* Linn. This butterfly is apparently distributed over the entire breadth of the Northern Hemisphere below the arctic circle, as far as the thirtieth parallel of latitude in America, and the fortieth in the old world. It is found in nearly equal abundance through all parts of New England, so numerous, indeed, as to become positively injurious on account of the damage done by the caterpillar to some of our choicest ornamental trees.

17. *Aglais Milberti* Scudd. This insect is found throughout New England, but is extremely rare in the southern portions. Probably the isotherm of 23° for the winter months would mark the limit of its abundance. It is rather common in Walpole, Dublin, Milford, and the Isles of Shoals. Still farther north it is very abundant, often the commonest species in its season, and is plentiful even in the White Mountain region itself.

18. *Vanessa Atalanta* Fabr. This butterfly enjoys a very extensive geographical range, extending over nearly the whole of the North American and European continents. I believe it is found plentifully, and in nearly equal numbers, through every part of New England, although there is no record of its capture in the heart of the White Mountain region. As the abundance of this species is more than ordinarily affected by the action of parasites, the records of a single year for any locality are comparatively valueless.

19. *Vanessa Huntera* Hübn. It is far more common in the southern than in the northern portions of New England, and is wholly wanting in the White Mountain district, although occurring as far north as Quebec. The northernmost localities from which it has been reported are Waterville, very few (Hamlin), and Norway, Me. (Smith), and Milford, N. H., scarce (Whitney).

20. *Vanessa cardui* Ochs. This insect, says Speyer,[*] "is the most widely distributed of all butterflies, and perhaps of all Lepidoptera. It inhabits the whole of Europe as far north as Lapland, the whole of Asia (with perhaps the exception of the polar regions), the whole of Africa, America from Hudson's bay to Brazil, and Australia; that is to say, all parts of the world, every zone, the northern as well as the southern hemisphere, its area of dispersion embracing little less than the whole globe. Moreover, in the warm regions it is by no means restricted to the higher altitudes, but inhabits the plains under the equator as well as in Lapland. It has therefore nowhere on the earth an inferior limit to its distribution, through excess of temperature or insufficiency of moisture. As to its upper limits, it is restricted only by the eternal snows of the loftiest mountains. It is, however, not yet determined whether it is found in the treeless regions of the arctic zone, as it is in the sub-glacial districts of the Alps." There is no spot in New England where it may not be found at certain seasons in abundance.

21. *Junonia Coenia* Hübn. In New England this is an exceedingly rare insect. Mr. Smith has seen several specimens from the vicinity of New Haven; Mr. McCurdy found it somewhat plentiful one autumn in the vicinity of Norwich, Conn.; Col. Higginson reports several from Newport, R. I.; and Mr. Bennett captured a single specimen at Springfield. Mr. Sanborn and myself have both taken specimens on Cape Cod. Dr. Harris took one specimen at Milton, Mass.; and I have captured a single individual at Hampton, N. H., the northernmost locality from which it has been reported in New England, or, indeed, in America.

22. *Speyeria Idalia* Scudd. Generally speaking this is not a common insect in New England, and is seldom seen above the annual isotherm of 45°. The most northerly stations from which it is recorded are Brunswick, Me. (Packard), Isles of Shoals, a few specimens, and Suncook, not common (Thaxter), Milford, common (Whitney), Dublin (Faxon), and Walpole, N. H. (Smith).

23. *Argynnis Cybele* God. In New England this insect is scarcely larger than *A. Aphrodite*, and the two species have frequently been confounded, but it is found throughout the whole area, excepting the White

Mountain region, and probably most of the country farther north. In the
northern half of the district it is uncommon, but in the extreme south
exceedingly abundant. The most northern known localities are Brunswick, Waterville, and Norway, Me.; and in New Hampshire, Isles of
Shoals (not common), Suncook (not common), Milford (very abundant),
Walpole, and Plymouth.

24. *Argynnis Aphrodite* God. In New England this is one of our
commonest butterflies, but it is wholly absent from the White Mountain
region, where it is replaced by the next species.

25. *Argynnis Atlantis* Edw. Abundant through all the cooler parts of
Canada, and very closely limited southwardly by the annual isotherm of
45°, only surpassing it in elevated regions and along mountain chains.
In New England it is probably common everywhere north of the isotherm
of 45° maximum temperature for the spring months, but is really abundant only in the White Mountain district, where it wholly replaces *A.
Aphrodite*. Other New Hampshire localities are Thornton, Shelburne
(Faxon, Minot), Littleton (Sanborn), Jefferson (Scudder), and even Suncook (Thaxter), Dublin (Faxon), and Milford, very rare (Whitney).

26. *Brenthis Myrina* Herr.-Schäff. This butterfly is found in nearly
equal abundance throughout New England, in the valleys of the White
Mountains, or by the sea-coast.

27. *Brenthis Montinus* Scudd. [Plate A., Fig. 1]. The geographical
range of this insect has been sufficiently indicated in the first part of this
paper, in the discussion of the sub-alpine zone. Very little can be added
to what has already been published concerning the seasons of this insect.
It has been found from July 21 to August 18. Specimens captured August
2 had well developed eggs; others taken August 11 were "in good con-
dition." It is therefore probable, from analogy with the other species of
the genus inhabiting New England, that the butterflies first appear in the
middle or latter part of June, and lay their eggs about the middle of
August; that these hatch at once, and that the embryonic caterpillars
hibernate, reviving sufficiently in the spring to undergo their changes
and appear on the wing in June. Perhaps, however, some of these caterpillars become lethargic and transform later, so as to appear on the
wing in August (while the June butterflies are laying their eggs), for
fresh individuals have been captured on August 11. Should observers

find females at this date with undeveloped eggs, this theory would seem more plausible, and might throw some light on the origin of the vernal series in the other species. It should be added that, in Europe, only one brood has been observed among the mountain species of this genus.

Probably no collector has seen more than eight or ten of these butterflies in a day's scramble among the mountains, but if sought early in July they might be found in greater abundance. They fly close to the ground among the scanty foliage growing in the rocky crevices of the steep mountain slopes. Messrs. Sanborn and Whitney have often seen them on the mountain willow, *Salix herbacea* Linn., which grows but a few inches above the ground. So frequent and prolonged were their visitations to this plant, that these observers sought carefully but in vain for eggs. It is more probable that the caterpillar feeds upon some of the Violaceæ.

28. *Brenthis Bellona* Herr.-Schäff. In New England this butterfly appears to be as well distributed and as common as *B. Myrina*, although elsewhere it is considered somewhat less abundant.

29. *Phyciodes Tharos* Kirb. In New England this species is almost everywhere exceedingly abundant. It is not uncommon even in the White Mountain district; but Mr. Smith, who has collected largely in Norway, Me., writes that he has never seen a dozen specimens there.

30. *Charidryas Nycteis* Scudd. In New England this is a very rare insect. Mr. Sanborn has found a single specimen in the Glen, at the base of the White Mountains, and Mr. Smith one at Walpole. The general distribution of this insect leads us to anticipate its occurrence anywhere in the southern half of New Hampshire.

31. *Limnæcia Harrisii* Scudd. Specimens of the imago have been taken among the White Mountains, and the sides of the Glen road swarm with the caterpillars at the proper season. It has also been found at Pittsfield (Treat), Dublin (Faxon), and Milford, rare and local (Whitney). It seems to be more common in the elevated and northern districts than elsewhere, and has seldom been found outside of the state.

32. *Euphydryas Phaeton* Scudd. This butterfly is so eminently local in its habits that it has not yet been found over the extent of country which it probably occupies. In New England it is found abundantly everywhere, from the heart of the White Mountains to the lower portion

of the Connecticut river valley, but, owing to its local habits, it is ordinarily esteemed rare. It occurs only in moist, or moist and shady, meadows of small extent. When young, it feeds on *Chelone glabra;* after hibernating, on *Lonicera ciliata.*

33. *Libythea Bachmanii* Kirtl. Two specimens of this butterfly have been taken at Littleton by Dr. F. F. Hodgman. With a single exception, this is the only known instance of its occurrence in New England.

RURALES.

34. *Thecla Liparops* LeC. This butterfly appears to be found throughout New England, although everywhere considered a rare species. In New Hampshire it has only been reported from Mt. Moriah, Thornton (Faxon), and Milford (Whitney).

35. *Thecla Edwardsii* Saund. Has been taken only in the extreme southern parts of the state, Milford (Whitney) and Nashua (Harris).

36. *Thecla Calanus* Doubl. This butterfly seems to occur throughout New England. In New Hampshire, it is very common at Walpole (Smith), but is probably absent from the northern and perhaps the central parts of the state, although it occurs at Norway, Me.

37. *Thecla acadica* Edw. This butterfly is rather widely distributed in New England. In New Hampshire it has been taken only at Milford, "very rare" (Whitney), and at Nashua (Harris).

38. *Calliparens Melinus* Scudd. A widely spread species that will probably be found in every part of the United States. In New England it is more abundant in the south than in the north, although it has been taken as far north as Norway, Me., and Plymouth, N. H. Other localities in New Hampshire are Dublin (Faxon), Suncook (Thaxter), and Milford (Whitney).

39. *Incisalia Augustus* Min. The distribution of this insect seems to be somewhat peculiar. Apparently reaching its maximum of development in New England, it occurs also in the Canadian fauna, even as far as the Cumberland house on the Saskatchawan, nearly in the centre of the continent, and has been described from California as a distinct species. Yet notwithstanding its occurrence in California, it has not otherwise been reported in the United States west of Albany. In New England it is widely distributed, and will probably be found in abundance all over

the wilder portion. It has not been reported from the White Mountains, and its northernmost known station is Norway, Me., very common (Smith). In Milford, N. H., it is rather uncommon (Whitney).

40. *Incisalia Niphon* Min. In New England this butterfly has been found in widely separated localities, more abundantly at the south than at the north. It has been taken in Norway, Me. (Smith), the White Mountains (Sanborn), and Milford, N. H., common (Whitney).

41. *Incisalia Irus* Scudd. The only known locality for this butterfly in New Hampshire is Milford, where it is scarce (Whitney).

42. *Strymon Titus* Butl. In New England it is considered a rare insect, but has occasionally been found in considerable numbers, and is well distributed at least over the southern portions. The only northern locality in which it has been found is Norway, Me., where it occurs in abundance (Smith). In New Hampshire it has been taken only at Milford, not common (Whitney).

43. *Cyaniris neglecta* Scudd. This butterfly is found across the continent. We may therefore naturally presume that it is found throughout New England. It is common in the southern half, but it is not often reported from the northern portions; perhaps, however, this is rather due to the lack of observers. Our northernmost recorded localities are Norway, Me. (Smith), and Dublin, N. H., "quite plenty" (Faxon).

44. *Cyaniris violacea* Scudd. This is by no means an uncommon insect in New England, but has generally been mistaken for one of the other species (coming, as it does, midway between neglecta and Lucia), on account of the absence in New England of the dark form of the female. Probably it will prove comparatively rare in the northern half. It has been taken at Walpole and Milford.

45. *Cyaniris Lucia* Scudd. This is an abundant insect throughout the northern half of New England, and cannot be called very uncommon even in Massachusetts.

46. *Everes Comyntas* Scudd. is found throughout New England, even in the White Mountain district, and is everywhere a common insect, especially in the southern half.

47. *Chrysophanus Hyllus* Hübn. In New England it has never been taken east of the Connecticut valley; and in New Hampshire only at Walpole, a single specimen (Smith).

48. *Chrysophanus epixanthe* Westw. In New England this butterfly has only been found east of the Connecticut valley. In New Hampshire it has been taken at Milford, very plentiful in a few localities (Whitney), Suncook, not common (Thaxter), and Hampton, abundant (Scudder).

49. *Lycæna americana* Harr. It is found throughout New England, almost as abundantly in the White Mountain district as elsewhere, and is one of our commonest species.

50. *Feniseca Tarquinius* Grote. The latitudinal distribution of this butterfly is greater than that of any other of the American coppers, since it is found from beyond the limits of the Alleghanian fauna on the north to the shores of the Gulf of Mexico. In New Hampshire it has been taken at Berlin Falls, Thornton, "very abundant below the cascade on Mill brook" (Faxon), Waterville, Manchester, and Milford.

PAPILIONIDÆ.

51. *Colias Philodice* God. In New England this butterfly is everywhere the commonest species, except in certain years, when it seems to be affected by some unfavorable circumstances. It is found alike in the White Mountain region and on the shores of the Sound, but is more abundant in the southern than in the northern districts.

52. *Eurema Lisa* Kirb. This butterfly is a member of the Carolinian fauna, where it is very abundant. A single specimen has been taken by Mr. Thaxter at the Isles of Shoals.

53. *Ganoris rapæ* Dalm. This butterfly is our most recent and least desirable importation from the old world, and before many years it will doubtless spread over the whole northern hemisphere. It was introduced at Quebec, and has rapidly spread southward and westward. The first specimens taken near New Hampshire were captured by Mr. Merrill, at Waterbury, Vt., in August, 1867; yet it was only in May of the same year that they appeared at Montreal. In August, 1868, they were not uncommon at Island Pond, on the Grand Trunk Railway, and the succeeding year were taken in July by Mr. Sanborn, at Littleton, and by Mr. Whorf, at Shelburne, and, in August, as far south as Campton, by the latter gentleman. It was not until September of the same year that they were discovered at Norway, Me., a few miles from Shelburne; and yet they were taken at Waterville, in the same state, in May of that year,

and still farther south, at Lewiston, even in the previous year! In 1870, the vanguard of the army crossed the state, reaching Milford in May, but they had even then penetrated as far as Springfield, in their march down the Connecticut, and were abundant at Walpole. They swarm now in every part of the state, not even excepting the Isles of Shoals, where Mr. Thaxter found them in 1870, and the alpine zone of the White Mountains, where I took fresh specimens in 1873.

54. *Ganoris oleracea* Scudd. [Plate A, Fig. 8.] It is found throughout New England, although seldom abundant south of the annual isotherm of 48°. Northward and eastward it is everywhere abundant, and continues to be so as far south as Williamstown, Mass., Dublin, N. H., and Portland, Me. It rarely occurs south of the northern boundary of Connecticut.

55. *Laertias Philenor* Hübn. [Plate A, Fig. 15, chrysalis, side view. Fig. 17, ib., dorsal view.] In New England this butterfly is very rare. In no locality has more than a single specimen been taken during a season, excepting near New Haven; one was taken and another seen by Mr. Smith, at Walpole, N. H., in 1870.

56. *Pterourus Troilus* Scudd. In New England this insect is not uncommon in the three southern states, and has been found north of Massachusetts, at Milford, not as common as Polyxenes (Whitney), Dublin (Faxon), and Walpole, N. H. (Smith), and at Sudbury, Vt., scarce (Scudder).

57. *Euphœades Glaucus* Hübn. [Plate A, Fig. 16.] This butterfly is more widely distributed than any other of our swallow-tails, for it is found in nearly every part of North America, from the Atlantic to the Pacific, from Newfoundland to northern Florida, and from central Alaska to California. Its northern limit in the eastern half of the continent closely follows the dividing line between the Canadian and Huronian faunas, as laid down by Allen. In New England it is everywhere common, from the summit of Mt. Washington to Long Island sound, but is more abundant in the northern than in the southern districts. In the White Mountain region it is exceedingly abundant, and individuals are often dusky and small, like those from Alaska.

58. *Amaryssus Polyxenes* Scudd. This insect is rather uniformly common throughout New England, although not mentioned by Gosse

among the butterflies of Compton, Lower Canada, which is rather strange, since it is found in the valleys of the White Mountains.

URBICOLÆ.

59. *Epargyreus Tityrus* Scudd. This is a tolerably common, sometimes abundant species in the three southern New England states, occurring even in the elevated portions. North of this it becomes rare, having been taken in New Hampshire only at Milford, "plenty" (Whitney), Dover (Faxon), Walpole (Smith), and Plymouth (Scudder).

60. *Achalarus Lycidas* Scudd. This is a rare insect in New England. It has occasionally occurred in abundance in New Haven and vicinity, and a few specimens are reported at rare intervals in various parts of Massachusetts. Mr. Whitney has taken three or four specimens at Milford, the northernmost known locality for this insect.

61. *Thorybes Pylades* Scudd. It is found in abundance in every part of New England.

62. *Erynnis Persius* Scudd. In New England it is everywhere common, from the valleys of the White Mountains and Norway, Me., to Cape Cod, Norwich, and New Haven.

63. *Erynnis Lucilius* Scudd. This insect has not been recorded from New Hampshire; but I have found empty nests of the larva among the leaves of Aquilegia in Plymouth, which must have been made by this species.

64. *Erynnis Icelus* Scudd. It is widely spread over New England, having been taken at nearly every place where there are resident collectors. In the north it has been found in the wilds of Maine, at Norway in the same state, in the valleys, and even in the sub-alpine zone of the White Mountains, at Plymouth, and farther south at Milford.

65. *Erynnis Brizo* Scudd. This, too, is widely spread in New England, but has not yet been found in the White Mountain valleys, although it has been taken at Waterville, Me., and Thornton, N. H. It has also been reported from Dublin and Milford, in the southern part of New Hampshire.

66. *Erynnis Juvenalis* Scudd. This butterfly is confined in New England to the three southern states, having been taken north of them in but a single locality (Milford, N. H.), where it is reported rare.

67. *Pholisora Catullus* Scudd. In New England this is not an uncommon insect in some southern localities, notably along the Connecticut river. Its northernmost recorded locality is Milford, N. H., very rare (Whitney).

68. *Ancyloxypha Numitor* Feld. In New England this smallest of our butterflies is abundant south of the latitude of $42°$ $30'$, but has been recorded from only a single locality north of it, Milford, N. H. As it is said to be common there, it will probably be found somewhat farther north.

69. *Amblyscirtes vialis* Scudd. In New England this butterfly is strictly limited to the southern half, having been found but once north of Massachusetts, at Milford, N. H. (Whitney).

70. *Amblyscirtes Samoset* Scudd. In New England it is found in such northern and elevated localities as Norway, Me., and the valleys of the White Mountains. It has also been taken at Milford, and once only in Massachusetts.

71. *Cyclopides Mandan* Scudd. In New England this butterfly has been taken but twice,—once in Norway, Me. (Smith), and once in the Glen, White Mountains (Sanborn).

72. *Oxytes Metea* Scudd. This is another of the many southern butterflies, whose northernmost known limit is Milford, N. H.

73. *Poanes Massasoit* Scudd. Excepting in New England this butterfly has not been taken north of Albany; in New England, although otherwise confined to the more southern portions, and especially to the lower levels, it has been taken at Milford, N. H.

74. *Atrytone Zabulon* Scudd. This common butterfly is taken throughout New England, in the southern parts of which it is exceedingly abundant. It is even common in such northern and elevated localities as Williamstown, Mass., Norway, Me., and Thornton and Plymouth, N. H.; it extends to Quebec and Nova Scotia.

75. *Pamphila Sassacus* Kirb. This butterfly occurs everywhere in the southern half of New England, but, excepting at Norway, Me., has not been taken in the northern half. Mr. Whitney has found it at Milford.

76. *Anthomaster Leonardus* Scudd. This butterfly also is confined in New England to the southern half, the northernmost localities from which it is recorded being Dublin (Faxon) and Milford, N. H. (Whitney).

77. *Polites Peckius* Scudd. In New England it is everywhere the commonest of the Astyci, and is found throughout every portion of the district, from the White Mountains to the sea-coast.

78. *Hedone Ætna* Scudd. It is found in the southern half of New England; once, however, a specimen was taken in Norway, Me. With that exception, its northernmost range is indicated by its capture in Walpole and Milford, N. H.

79. *Limochores Mystic* Scudd. It is found everywhere in New England, from the White Mountains to Cape Cod and New Haven. There is hardly a local collection of any size that does not contain it.

80. *Limochores bimacula* Scudd. It has seldom been taken in New England, and never north of Massachusetts, except at Milford, N. H., where it is rare.

81. *Limochores Manataaqua* Scudd. In New England it has been found only in widely separated localities. Among these, and one of the most northern, is Walpole, N. H., where Mr. Smith found it somewhat common.

82. *Limochores Taumas* Scudd. This butterfly is found over perhaps a larger extent of territory than any other species of its tribe. In New England it is everywhere common, from the White Mountains, and even from its highest altitudes, to the southern and eastern sea-coast.

83. *Euphyes Metacomet* Scudd. This insect is widely spread in New England, although it has been taken but rarely in its northern half; it has been taken at Norway, Me., and Thornton, N. H., and is not uncommon at Plymouth, Walpole, and Milford. South of these latter points it is everywhere rather common and sometimes abundant.

84. *Euphyes verna* Scudd. In New England it is confined to the Alleghanian region, and is everywhere exceedingly rare. A single specimen has been taken at Milford by Mr. Whitney.

85. *Lerema Hianna* Scudd. This member of the Alleghanian fauna has thus far been detected in New England in only a few localities. It is confined to its southern portions, but has been found to be somewhat common at Milford by Mr. Whitney.

III. LIST OF THE ORTHOPTERA OF NEW HAMPSHIRE, WITH NOTES ON THEIR GEOGRAPHICAL DISTRIBUTION AND STRIDULATION.

In the following pages I have given a list of all the species known to me to inhabit the state, adding notes upon their geographical distribution both within and without the state. Such information is given concerning the mode and character of their stridulation as could be obtained. Unfortunately most of the material for the list has been collected about the White Mountains only in excursions made by my friends and myself. This accounts for its poverty.

GRYLLIDES.

1. *Gryllotalpa borealis* Burm. [Plate A, Fig. 7.] The northern mole-cricket inhabits nearly the whole of the United States east of the great plains, from Louisiana to Massachusetts. It has not yet been discovered in New Hampshire, but it will doubtless be found in the southern portions of the state, as it is not at all uncommon in the region about Boston and Springfield, Mass., and has been taken by Prof. Verrill, at Anticosti. The figure has been introduced upon the plate, to call the attention of those interested, and because it is one of the most peculiar forms among Orthoptera. It is a burrowing insect, as the character of the forelegs readily indicates. At Winter pond, Winchester, Mass., the whole surface of the ground beneath the sod and stones for a rod from the water's edge is completely honeycombed with their burrows. They seldom penetrate to a depth of more than six or eight inches, rarely to a foot beneath the surface. The burrows are usually about a third of an inch in diameter, entirely irregular in direction, and often terminate abruptly. Where the ground is hard the burrows are brought so near the surface as to raise long ridges of mould, which, when dry, frequently fall in and expose the burrows. The note of this insect is most frequently heard at dusk, and resembles the distant sound of frogs, but is somewhat feebler.

2. *Gryllus luctuosus* Serv. This insect is readily distinguished from all other species of the genus found in this part of the country by the great length of the wings, which extend far beyond the body and the elytra. It has been taken in New Hampshire by Mrs. F. W. Putnam, and is not infrequent even so far north as the valleys of the White Mountains. The individuals from this locality are much smaller than farther south.

Other species of this genus doubtless occur in New Hampshire, but I do not happen to possess specimens for determination. At Jefferson, in 1867, no chirp of a Gryllus was heard until August 12, although they often commence their song in Massachusetts in June.

3. *Nemobius vittatus* Harr. is found all over the state, even in the White Mountain region, and extends west as far as Nebraska, and south at least to Maryland. It appears a little earlier than the species of Gryllus, but in the White Mountains not until August. Its chirp is very similar to that of Gryllus, and can best be expressed by *ru* or *rruu*, pronounced as

Fig. 48.

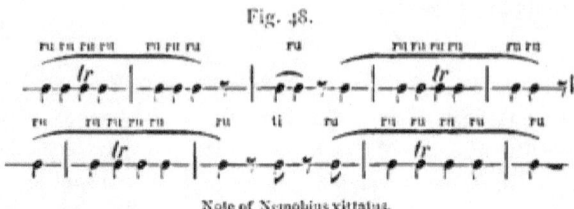

Note of Nemobius vittatus.

though it were a French word. The note is trilled forcibly, and lasts a variable length of time, sometimes for several seconds; at others it is reduced to a short, sharp click.*

I once observed one of these insects singing to its mate. At first the song was mild, and frequently broken; afterward it grew impetuous, forcible, and more prolonged; then it decreased in volume and extent till it became quite soft and feeble. At this time the male began to approach the female, uttering a series of twittering chirps; the female ran away, and the male, after a short chase, returned to his old haunt, singing with the same vigor as before, but with more frequent pauses; at last, finding all persuasion unavailing, he brought his serenade to a close. The pauses of his song were almost instantly followed by a peculiar jerk of the body; it consisted of an impulsive movement backward, and then as suddenly forward, and was accompanied by a corresponding movement of the antennæ together, and then apart. The female was near enough to be touched by the antennæ of the male during the first movement, and usually started in a nearly similar way as soon as touched.

The elytra of the male are held at an angle of about twenty degrees from the body during stridulation, and, perhaps, at a slightly greater angle from each other. Even when most violent, the sound is produced

* It is necessary for me to describe the peculiar system of musical notation which I have adopted. Each bar represents a second of time, and is occupied by the equivalent of a semibreve; consequently a quarter note (♪) or a quarter rest (♩) represents a quarter of a second; a sixteenth note (♬) or a sixteenth rest (♪) a sixteenth of a second, etc. For convenience' sake, I have introduced a new form of rest (▬ or ▬), which indicates silence through the remainder of a measure.

by the friction of the inner edges of the elytra only, not by the whole surface.

4. *Nemobius fasciatus* Scudd. This cricket may prove to be only a long-winged form of the preceding, as it scarcely differs from it in anything but the length of these organs. It is also found throughout New Hampshire, even in the White Mountain region. It occurs as far south as South Carolina, Louisiana, and Texas, and west at least to Missouri. I have not noticed any difference between the chirp of this species and of the preceding.

5. *Œcanthus niveus* Serv. is probably found in the southern portions of the state, although no record of its occurrence has fallen under my notice. It is certainly found in the neighboring parts of Massachusetts. This insect does great damage to young shoots of raspberry, blackberry, and even of the grape-vine, by depositing its eggs within the stem; these are laid in a nearly perpendicular row, often a foot long, at short distances apart, a single egg being introduced through each hole into the very heart of the stem, weakening it to such a degree that it is apt to break in a strong wind. A European species, thought by some to be identical with this, has a slightly different habit, and is far less, if at all, injurious. It makes its punctures much farther apart, and introduces two or three eggs into each opening.

The day-song of this insect is exceedingly shrill, and may be represented by the following figure, though the notes vary in rapidity. When

Fig. 49.

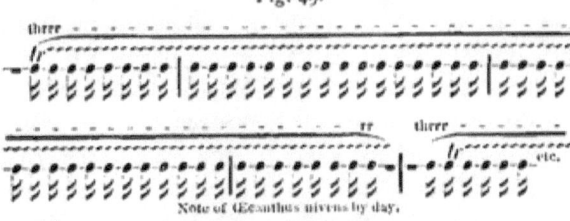

Note of Œcanthus niveus by day.

slowest they are about sixteen a second. The song is of varied length, sometimes lasting but two or three seconds, sometimes continuing a minute or two uninterruptedly; it is a nearly uniform, equally sustained trill, but the insect often commences its note at a different pitch from the normal one, as if it required a little practice to attain it. When singing, the tegmina are raised at fully a right angle to the body. The night-song consists of *thrrr* repeated incessantly, three parts of song and one of rest in every three seconds.

Fig. 50.

Note of Œcanthus niveus by night.

LOCUSTARIÆ.

6. *Ceuthophilus maculatus* Scudd. is found throughout New England and as far south as Maryland. I once took a specimen half way up Mt. Washington. All the Vermont specimens I have seen are unusually dark.

7. *Phylloptera oblongifolia* Burm. has not been found in the state, but as it occurs somewhat abundantly in Massachusetts, and is found as far west as Iowa, it doubtless inhabits at least the southern part of New Hampshire. I have not studied its note attentively, but if I recollect aright, it gives three rapid notes in succession like the katydid.

8. *Phaneroptera curvicauda* Serv. This insect is found all over the state, even inhabiting the sub-alpine zones of the White Mountains. It is found also as far south as the Carolinas, and west to the Red river settlements of British America, to Michigan, and Illinois. It is more noisy by night than by day; and the songs differ considerably at these two times. The day-song is given only during sunshine, the other by night and in cloudy weather. I first noticed this while watching one of these little creatures close beside me; as a cloud passed over the sun, he suddenly changed his note to one with which I was already familiar, but without knowing to what insect it belonged. At the same time, all the individuals around me whose similar day-song I had heard, began to respond with the night cry: the cloud passed away, and the original note was resumed on all sides. Judging that they preferred the night-song to that of the day, from their increased stridulation during the former period,

I imitated the night-song during sunshine, and obtained an immediate response in the same language. The experiment proved that the insects could hear as well as sing.

This species is exceedingly shy, and the observer must be patient who would hold converse with it. One insect which I had disturbed, and beside which I was standing, could not at first decide to resume his song; he was afraid of the intruder, but, enticed by a neighboring songster, gave

Fig. 51.

Note of Phaneroptera curvicauda by day.

utterance several times to a barely discernible, short click or *tt;* after five or six of these efforts his desires overcame his fears. The note by day is *bzrwt*, and lasts for one third of a second.

The night-song consists of a repetition, ordinarily eight times, of a note which sounds like *tchw.* It is repeated at the rate of five times in

Fig. 52.

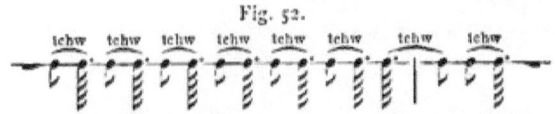

Note of Phaneroptera curvicauda by night.

three quarters of a second, making each note half the length of the day note.

9. *Conocephalus ensiger* Harr. Found throughout New England, even into the sub-alpine zone of the White Mountains; it extends south as far as the middle states and southern Illinois, and west to Nebraska, Minnesota, and the Red river of the north. Mr. Smith found a female of this insect "with the ovipositor forced down between the root-leaves and the stalk of the *Andropogon,* where the eggs are probably deposited."

There is a species of Conocephalus (*C. robustus* Scudd.), found on the southern sea-beaches of New England, which is exceedingly noisy, and sings equally, and, I believe, similarly, by day and night. The song resembles that of the harvest fly, *Cicada canicularis.* It often lasts for many minutes, and seems, at a distance, to be quite uniform; on a nearer approach, one can hear it swelling and decreasing in volume, while there is a corresponding muscular movement from the front of the abdomen backward, two and a half times a second. This is accompanied by a buzzing sound, quite audible near at hand; it resembles the humming of a bee, or the droning of a bagpipe.

C. ensiger also seems to have a single song, but it stridulates only by night or during cloudy weather; it commences its song as soon as the sky is obscured or the sun is near the horizon; it begins with a note like *brw*, then pauses an instant and immediately emits a rapid succession of sounds like *chwi* at the rate of about five per second, and continues them for an unlimited time. Either the rapidity of the notes is variable, becoming sometimes as frequent as twenty-three in three seconds, or else there is some deceptive character in its song. In a number of

Fig. 53.

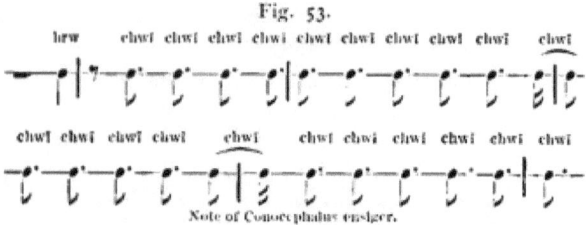

Note of Conocephalus ensiger.

instances I have counted the notes as rapid as the highest rate given above, but on a nearer approach to verify them the rate was invariably reduced to five per second; it is doubtful whether this was due to alarm at my approach, for this is the least shy of all our Locustarians.

10. *Xiphidium fasciatum* Serv. It is found from the valleys of the White Mountain region southward, as far as Maryland and southern Illinois. Its note resembles that of Orchelimum, but is exceedingly faint.

11. *Xiphidium brevipenne* Scudd. This species has much the same distribution as the preceding, but is not recorded from points so far south, although it reaches Pennsylvania and Michigan. One year its first appearance was recorded about Boston, July 16th; another year in the neighborhood of Jefferson, White Mountains, August 8th.

12. *Orchelimum vulgare* Harr. This insect is found through all the White Mountain region, even to the alpine zone, and also over the rest of the state. It is everywhere very abundant, as its name indicates. It is also found southward at least as far as Maryland and southern Illinois, probably also to the Carolinas. There is not so great disparity in the time

of its appearance in the White Mountain region and in southern New England, as in some other species. One year it appeared in Jefferson, July 28, and the following year about Boston, July 15.

Fig. 54.

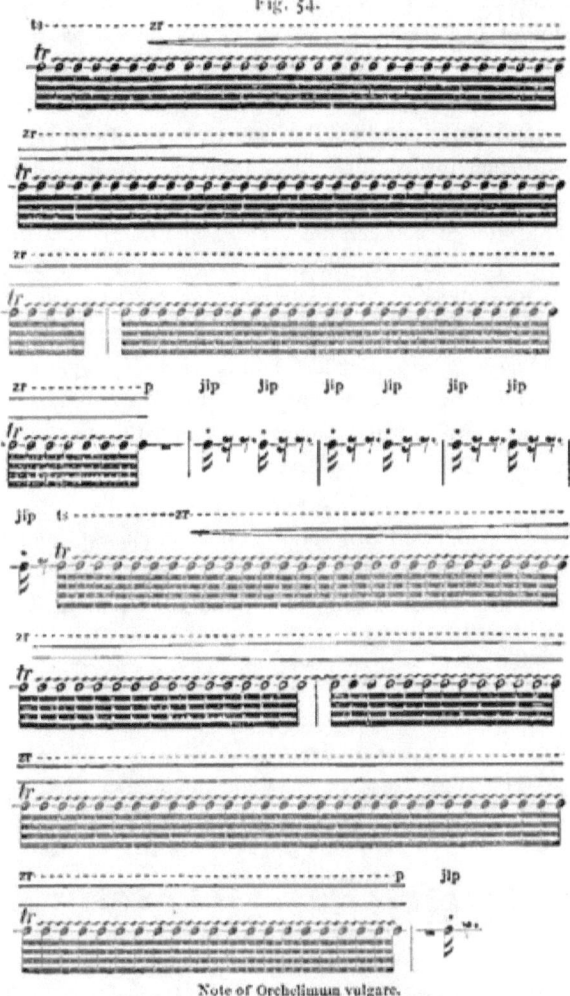

Note of Orcbelimum vulgare.

Its song is more complicated than that of our other Locustarians. Commencing with *ts*, it changes almost instantly into a trill of *zr;* at first there is a crescendo movement, which reaches its volume in half a second; the trill is then sustained for a period varying from one to twenty seconds (generally from six to eight seconds), and closes abruptly with *p*. This strain is followed by a series of very short staccato notes sounding like *jip!* repeated at half-second intervals; the staccato notes and the trill alternate *ad libitum*. The staccato notes *may* be continued almost indefinitely, but are very rarely heard more than ten times in succession; it ordinarily occurs three or four times before the repetition of the phrase, but not more than two or three times when the phrase is not repeated. I have known it to be entirely omitted, even before the repetition of a phrase. The interval between the last *jip!* and the recommencement of the phrase never exceeds one quarter of a second. The night-song differs from that of the day in the rarer occurrence of the immediate notes and the less rapid trill of the phrase; the pitch of both is at B flat.

13. *Thyreonotus dorsalis* Scudd. I have taken a single specimen of this insect as far north as Sudbury, Vt.; and since it also occurs in eastern Massachusetts, it will no doubt be found within the limits of New Hampshire in the Connecticut valley.

ACRYDII.

14. *Chloealtis conspersa* Harr. This is a northern insect, extending from Maine to Lake Winnipeg, and is found all over New Hampshire, even in the valleys of the White Mountains. South of the state it occurs on

Fig. 55.

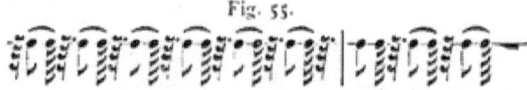

Note of Chloealtis conspersa in the sun.

high lands. The male differs so much in appearance from the female that I formerly described it under a distinct generic name. Its song is

Fig. 56.

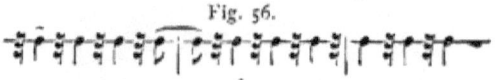

Note of Chloealtis conspersa in the shade.

of varied rapidity, according to the amount of sunshine; in the sun it makes from nine to twelve notes, at the rate of fifty-three in fifteen seconds; the usual number of notes is ten.

In the shade the rate falls to forty-three in fifteen seconds, the number of notes remaining the same.

The femur is evidently scraped gently upon the elytron to produce the sound, for frequently, at the commencement, two or three noiseless movements are made, the leg failing to touch the wing-cover. I once found three males singing to a single female, who was busily engaged laying eggs in a stick of wood, her abdomen plunged into a hole she had bored to the depth of half an inch; two of the males were near enough each other to cross antennæ.

Mr. S. I. Smith gives an interesting account of the habits of this species in the *Proceedings of the Portland* (Me.) *Society of Natural History.*

The eggs are deposited in old logs, in the under sides of boards, or in any soft wood lying among the grass which these insects inhabit. By means of the anal appendages, the female excavates in the wood a smooth, round hole, about an eighth of an inch in diameter. This hole is almost perpendicular at first, but is turned rapidly off in the direction of the grain of the wood, and runs nearly parallel with, and about three eighths of an inch from, the surface,—the whole length of the hole being an inch or an inch and a fourth. A single hole noticed in the end of a log was straight. The eggs, which are about a fourth of an inch in length, quite slender, and light brownish yellow, are placed in two rows, one on each side, and inclined so that, beginning at the end of the hole, each egg overlies the next in the same row by about half its length. The aperture is closed by a little disk of a hard, gummy substance. I have seen many of the females engaged in excavating the holes, and they always stood with the body in the direction of the grain of the wood, and apparently did not change their position during the operation. When one was just beginning a hole, it was very easy to see the upper appendages rise and open, and each time scrape away a little of the wood. During this operation a frothy fluid is emitted from some part of the abdomen, but whether it serves to soften the wood, or to lubricate the appendages and the sides of the hole, I did not determine. There were always great numbers of half finished holes, or those just begun, and comparatively very few that were completed; and I have often found upon the under side of boards great numbers of the holes just begun, none of them being more than an eighth of an inch in depth. Perhaps the reason for so few holes being finished is, that the wood proves too hard, and the insect tries for a softer place, or, many of them may be disturbed during the operation. When they had opened the hole only to a slight depth, they leaped away if disturbed; but when the abdomen was quite a distance into the nearly completed hole, they seldom attempted to withdraw it even after the hand was upon them.

I have also noticed that this insect is not easily suited in choosing the best place to bore her nest; the wood must be firm enough to retain the eggs well in place, and soft enough to absorb much moisture in the spring. Upright pieces of timber are never chosen, but rather short sticks of decaying, charred, or pithy wood, which cannot easily be broken or blown against the rocks. Holes are frequently made three quarters of an inch deep, and abandoned because the spot proves unsuitable. In a stick about a foot and a half long and two or three inches wide, I counted seventy-five borings, only three or four of which had been used as nests. The number of imperfect to perfect holes must be as twenty-five to one, or, perhaps, as fifty to one. When a good piece of wood is discovered, the nests are crowded thickly together; and a stick less than two inches in diameter and five inches in length contained thirteen completed nests. The holes are pierced at a slight angle to the perpendicular, away from the insect; they are straight for about a quarter of an inch, then turn abruptly and run horizontally along the grain for about an inch. The eggs (from ten to fourteen in number) are almost always laid in the horizontal portion of the nest; they are cylindrical, tapering toward the ends, but not at all pointed, and measure from five to five and a half millimetres in length, by one and one eighth in breadth; the ends are equally and regularly rounded. They vary in tint, some being almost colorless, and others of a faint yellow. After the eggs have been carefully packed away in the sawdust made by the abrasion of the sides of the hole, they are covered above with a whitish froth, and the hole is sealed up just below the surface of the wood with a black glutinous secretion, excessively hard, smooth, and shiny, and the upper surface slightly concave. In the spring the moisture doubtless softens these coverings so that the young grasshoppers can easily escape. Many old nests may be found uncovered and filled with the shells of the eggs, but none in which the cover is still retained.

15. *Chrysochraon viridis* Thom. This grasshopper has been taken in southern New Hampshire; it has an extensive range, having been taken, according to Thomas, as far west as southern Illinois and Nebraska.

16. *Stenobothrus curtipennis* Scudd. A very common species all over the state and in the valleys of the White Mountains; it extends from Maine to the Red river settlements in British America, and thence southward to Pennsylvania, southern Illinois, Colorado, and Wyoming. It

inhabits uplands rather than moist grounds. When about to stridulate, these insects place themselves in a nearly horizontal position, with the head a little elevated; they then raise both hind legs at once, and grate the thighs against the outer surface of the elytra. The first one or two movements are frequently noiseless or faint. In sunny weather the notes

Fig. 57.

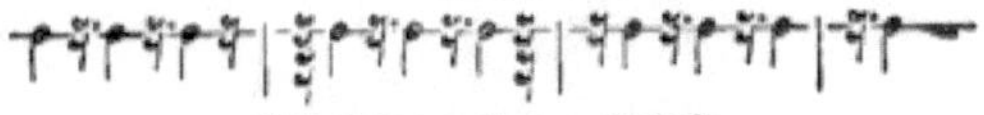

Note of Stenobothrus curtipennis.

are produced at the rate of about six a second, and are continued from one and a half to two and a half seconds. When the sky is overcast, the movements are less rapid.

17. *Stenobothrus maculipennis* Scudd. The range of this insect is similar to that of the preceding. It is found in the White Mountain valleys and all over the state. Also, westward as far as Minnesota, Wyoming, and Nebraska.

18. *Stenobothrus æqualis* Scudd. This insect is believed by Smith to be identical with the preceding, and may prove to be. It also occurs in the White Mountain valleys and in other parts of New Hampshire, and has been taken in Maine, Massachusetts, New York, the middle states, and Minnesota.

19. *Tragocephala infuscata* Harr. A wide-spread insect, not only found in every part of the state, including the valleys of the White Mountain region, and up at least to the sub-alpine zone, but reaching southward to North Carolina and Louisiana, and westward to Nebraska and Colorado.

20. *Tragocephala sordida* Stål. This grasshopper is found in the southern half of the state, and extends from Maine, in the latitude of the White Mountains, to Maryland and Tennessee in the south, and Nebraska, Iowa, and Minnesota in the west. It has also been taken at London, Ontario, Canada.

21. *Arcyptera lineata* Scudd. This grasshopper has not been taken in the state, but, having been found at Norway, Me., Williamstown and Andover, Mass., it doubtless occurs here. It has also been taken in the valley of the Red river of the north.

22. *Arcyptera gracilis* Scudd. · This insect is abundant at Jefferson

and other parts of the White Mountains, and is common on the summit of Graylock in Massachusetts; it has also been taken at Norway and other parts of Maine, and in Minnesota, and is abundant in the Red river settlements of British America. It is a very shy insect, but stridulates more loudly than other Acridians; its note can be heard at a distance of fifty feet. It usually makes four notes, but the number is sometimes greater. The first, a quarter of a second in length, is duller than the

Fig. 58.

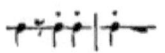

Note of Arcyptera gracilis.

others, and is followed by a pause of a quarter second; the other notes are of the same length, but sharply sounded and follow each other rapidly.

23. *Pezotettix borealis* Scudd. This northern insect, originally described from Minnesota, the Saskatchawan river, Lake Winnipeg, and the Island of Anticosti, has since been mentioned from Speckled mountain in Stoneham, Me., and occurs also among the White Mountains. It is thought by some to be identical with *P. frigida* of northern Europe.

24. *Pezotettix manca* Smith. Described from a single specimen taken on Speckled mountain, Stoneham, Me.; doubtless, therefore, it will be found in the hilly parts of New Hampshire.

25. *Pezotettix glacialis* Scudd. [Plate A, Figs. 5, 10.] I have found this wingless Acridian most plentifully on Mt. Madison, the neighborhood of the snow-bank in Tuckerman's ravine, and at the ledge, all within the sub-alpine zone. In the latter place it frequents the branches of the small birch trees. I am not aware that any other of our Acridians are found habitually upon trees. I have found this species on Graylock (Berkshire county), Mass. Mr. Sanborn has taken it about the Umbagog lakes in northern Maine, and Mr. Smith on Speckled mountain, Stoneham, Me. Of this latter locality Mr. Smith says,—"It is in the southwestern part of Oxford county, and probably belongs to the White Mountain group. I am not aware that its height has ever been determined, but it is probably not much above two thousand feet. Upon the upper and treeless part of the mountain, where all the species of Pezotettix occurred [see the two preceding species], the following plants were abundant:

Alsine grænlandica Fenzl., *Potentilla tridentata* Ait., *Vaccinium Vitis-Idæa* Linn., *V. uliginosum* Linn., *Empetrum nigrum* Linn."

26. *Melanoplus femur-rubrum* Stål. This species is wide-spread and destructive; it is found over all the portions of the United States lying east of the Rocky Mountains, excepting perhaps those bordering the Gulf of Mexico. In New Hampshire it ascends to the tops of the highest mountains, being common in both the alpine and sub-alpine zones. It has at times migrated in swarms like its congener, *M. spretus*, one of the most devastating of all insects. "The southern and western parts of New Hampshire," says Dr. Harris, in his treatise on injurious insects, "have been overrun by swarms of these grasshoppers, and have suffered more or less from their depredations." Dr. True gives the following account of their ravages in Pownal (Cumberland county), Me., about half a century ago:

During the haying season the weather was dry and hot, and these hungry locusts stripped the leaves from the clover and herds-grass, leaving nothing but the naked stems. In consequence, the hay crop was seriously diminished in value. So ravenous had they become that they would attack clover, eating it into shreds. Rake and pitchfork handles, made of white ash, and worn to a glossy smoothness by use, would be found nibbled over by them if left within their reach.

As soon as the hay was cut, and they had eaten every living thing from the ground, they removed to the adjacent crops of grain, completely stripping the leaves; climbing the naked stalks, they would eat off the stems of wheat and rye just below the head, and leave them to drop to the ground. I well remember assisting in sweeping a large cord over the heads of wheat after dark, causing the insects to drop to the ground, where most of them would remain during the night. During harvest time it was my painful duty, with a younger brother, to pick up the fallen wheat heads for threshing; they amounted to several bushels.

Their next attack was upon the Indian corn and potatoes. They stripped the leaves and ate out the silk from the corn, so that it was rare to harvest a full ear. Among forty or fifty bushels of corn spread out in the corn-room, not an ear could be found not mottled with detached kernels.

While these insects were more than usually abundant in the town generally, it was in the field I have described that they appeared in the greatest intensity. After they had stripped everything from the field, they began to emigrate in countless numbers. They crossed the highway and attacked the vegetable garden. I remember the curious appearance of a large, flourishing bed of red onions, whose tops they first literally ate up, and, not content with that, devoured the interior of the bulbs, leaving the dry external covering in place. The provident care of my mother, who covered the bed with chaff from the stable floor, did not save them, while she was complimented the next year for so successfully sowing the garden down to grass. The leaves were stripped from the apple-trees. They entered the house in swarms, reminding one of the locusts of Egypt, and, as we walked, they would rise in countless numbers and fly away in clouds.

As the nights grew cooler they collected on the spruce and hemlock stumps and log fences, completely covering them, eating the moss and decomposed surface of the wood, and leaving the surface clean and new. They would perch on the west side of a stump, where they could feel the warmth of the sun, and work around to the east side in the morning as the sun reappeared. The foot-paths in the fields were literally covered with their excrements.

During the latter part of August and the first of September, when the air was still dry, and for several days in succession a high wind prevailed from the north-west, the locusts frequently rose in the air to an immense height. By looking up at the sky in the middle of a clear day, as nearly as possible in the direction of the sun, one may descry a locust at a great height. These insects could thus be seen in swarms, appearing like so many thistle-blows, as they expanded their wings and were borne along toward the sea before the wind; myriads of them were drowned in Casco bay, and I remember hearing that they frequently dropped on the decks of coasting vessels. Cart-loads of dead bodies remained in the fields, forming in spots a tolerable coating of manure.

27. *Melanoplus punctulatus (Caloptenus punctulatus* Uhl.). This insect having been taken in Maine and in central Vermont, must occur in parts of New Hampshire.

28. *Melanoplus bivittatus (Gryllus bivittatus* Say). One may find this insect almost anywhere in New Hampshire, perched on the huge leaves of *Inula Helenium* growing by road-sides. It occurs in the White Mountain valleys, and has a very wide distribution extending along the Atlantic coast from Maine to Carolina or Georgia, and westward to the Rocky Mountains, where, Thomas says, it "is found east of the range from New Mexico to Montana [and farther, for I have taken it on Lake Winnipeg, and Kirby took it in latitude 65°, or about Fort Simpson in Arctic America], and west of it from Salt lake north to the dead waters of Snake river; and, although it is not mentioned among the collections made in Washington territory, yet I am of the opinion it will be found there."

29. *Œdipoda carolina* Burm. This grasshopper is found through all the parts of the state included in the Alleghanian fauna, but no farther; it is found, for instance, at Shelburne, on the Androscoggin, but not in the Glen, or the upper valley of the Peabody. It is a wide-spread species,

reaching Georgia and Mississippi on the south, and extending westward to New Mexico, Colorado, Nebraska, Utah, Wyoming, and even, according to Walker, Vancouver's island, on the Pacific coast. It makes a muffled, rustling sound with its wings during a somewhat sustained flight.

30. *Hippiscus phœnicopterus (Œdipoda phœnicoptera* Germ.). Plymouth is the only place in New Hampshire in which I have taken this grasshopper, but it doubtless occurs in all the region south of the White Mountains, for it is found throughout the southern part of New England, and as far south as Carolina, and even Florida, and, according to Thomas and Walker, reaches Colorada, Dakota, and Nebraska.

31. *Hippiscus rugosus (Œdipoda rugosa* Scudd.). This grasshopper has not yet been captured in New Hampshire, but it undoubtedly belongs to the fauna of the state, having been taken in Norway, Me., upon one side, and Massachusetts on the other, and also, according to Thomas, in the distant regions of Nebraska, Dakota, and Missouri.

32. *Arphia xanthoptera (Œdipoda xanthoptera* Germ.). Extends from middle New Hampshire to Carolina along the Atlantic coast, and westward to the Mississippi.

33. *Arphia sulphurea* Stål. Although this insect has never been recorded from New Hampshire, it doubtless inhabits the state, for it is found in Norway, Me., and is not at all uncommon in Massachusetts; it is, however, a southern insect, extending to Florida, and westward to Colorado, Missouri, and Nebraska, according to Thomas, and even, by Mr. Walker's statement, to Vancouver's island, on the Pacific coast.

34. *Trimerotropis æqualis (Gryllus æqualis* Say). This grasshopper is found at Norway, Me., and, as it occurs also in Vermont and Massachusetts, it must belong to the fauna of New Hampshire. According to Walker, it extends south to Florida; but I know of it from no point farther south than Long island. Westward, I have taken it at the Red river settlements and Minnesota, and it also occurs in Iowa, Dakota, and northern Illinois.

35. *Trimerotropis verruculata (Locusta verruculata* Kirb.). A very abundant species in the valleys of the White Mountains, as well as all over the state; it has also been taken on the top of Mts. Tom and Graylock in Massachusetts, in the northern wilds of Maine, on the Saguenay river in Canada, the region of the Saskatchawan river, and even in south-

ern Illinois, the only southern locality I know; at least, Mr. Thomas sent
it to me from there: could he have received it from some other quarter?
This insect, like the preceding, stridulates at will during flight; the flight
is well sustained, and the insect is capable of changing its course. At
each turn it accompanies the movement with a swoop-like curve, and

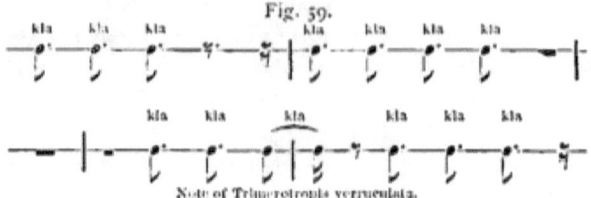

Note of Trimerotropis verruculata.

emits a crackling sound. In verruculata the sound is like *kl* or *kla*, the
former at a distance, the latter nearer by; it is repeated at the rate of
about five per second. Just before alighting, it crackles more rapidly
and frequently.

36. *Trimerotropis maritima* Stål. This curious grasshopper is a good
example of mimicry, for it so closely resembles the color of the sand on
a sea-beach that it is difficult to see it when alighted. It is found only
in such localities, and reaches its northern limits about the narrow part
of the state washed by the sea. I have taken it at Hampton. Southward it extends at least as far as New Jersey.

37. *Camnula pellucida (Œdipoda pellucida* Scudd.) This insect is
silent in flight, and is a northern species, swarming in immense numbers
among the White Mountains and on the dry summits of the country
south of it. The top of Mt. Prospect, near Plymouth, was covered with
myriads of them in the autumn of 1873. It is found, however, as far
south as Connecticut and southern Illinois, and west to the latter region
and Lake Superior. It is very closely allied to *C. atrox* of the Pacific
coast, which is said to be the most destructive grasshopper there, and to
migrate in swarms like *Melanoplus spretus.*

38. *Tettix granulata* Scudd. This is a northern insect, occurring
throughout the state, even into the valleys of the White Mountains.
Southward it extends as far as the middle states, but is most common
farther north; it occurs at Hudson's bay and about Lake Huron, and as
far west as Minnesota. Kirby took it in Arctic America, as far north
as lat. 65°, probably near Fort Simpson.

39. *Tettix ornata* Scudd.   This more southern species is still found in New Hampshire, at least in the southern portion; other northern localities are Norway, Me., and Royalton, Vt.   It extends southward as far as the District of Columbia, southern Illinois, and eastern Missouri.

40. *Tettix triangularis* Scudd.   This species, which also occurs in southern New Hampshire, seems to have a distribution very similar to that of the preceding, having also been taken in Maine, and extending as far south as the middle states; it does not seem to have been noticed far west, but has been taken at Prescott, Canada West.

41. *Tettigidea lateralis* Scudd.   Also a southern species, but found in southern New Hampshire, and in Maine as far north as Norway.   Southward, it extends to Florida, and westward to southern Illinois and the vicinity of St. Louis.

42. *Tettigidea polymorpha* Scudd.   The distribution of this species is apparently identical with that of the preceding.   It is found in southern New Hampshire and in Maine as far as Norway, where it is said to be common; southward it is recorded as far as Alabama, and west to Prescott, Canada West, southern Illinois, and the vicinity of St. Louis, Mo.

43. *Batrachidea cristata* Scudd.   This species has apparently a more limited range.   It is recorded from New Hampshire, but from what portion of it is unknown; in Maine it has been taken in the centre of the state, and at Norway "on rocky hills."   Southward it extends to the middle states, but is not mentioned from any point farther west.

PHASMIDA.

44. *Diapheromera femorata* Scudd. [Plate A, Fig. 3.]   The walking-stick appears to be rare north of Massachusetts; it has, however, been taken in New Hampshire, and I have found it as far north as Sudbury, Vt., and even in the Red river settlements in British America.   It has also been taken in Prescott, Canada West, and extends as far west as Nebraska, Kansas, and Iowa, and southward to Virginia, and, judging from poor specimens, from the farther parts of Texas.   It lives mostly upon the lower branches of oaks, or on young trees of less than a man's height.   The eggs are dropped loosely upon the ground, and do not hatch until the succeeding year, sometimes not until the second year.

BLATTARIE.

45. *Phyllodromia germanica* Serv.   This cosmopolitan pest, well known

as the "water bug," has been taken in New Hampshire; it undoubtedly reached this country from Europe.

Doubtless other species of this family occur upon the seaboard, but none have been recorded.

FORFICULARIÆ.

46. *Labia minuta* Scudd. Smith records the capture of a number of specimens of this earwig at Norway, Me., and we may therefore conclude that it inhabits New Hampshire, for it occurs southwardly as far as Maryland, where Mr. Uhler found it in rotten fungi, and even Virginia. It has not been found west of the Atlantic states. Dohrn considers it identical with the European *L. minor*.

EXPLANATION OF PLATE A.

Fig. 1. Brenthis Montinus.
 "   2. Œneis semidea.
 "   3. Diapheromera femorata.
 "   4. Œ. semidea; chrysalis, dorsal view.
 "   5. Pezotettix glacialis, side view.
 "   6. Œ. semidea; chrysalis, side view.
 "   7. Gryllotalpa borealis.
 "   8. Ganoris oleracea.
 "   9. Œ. semidea; hinder extremity of caterpillar, from above; enlarged.
 "   10. P. glacialis, dorsal view.
 "   11. Œ. semidea; front view of head of caterpillar; enlarged.
 "   12. Polygonia Progne.
 "   13. Œ. semidea; caterpillar, side view.
 "   14. Œ. semidea; caterpillar, dorsal view.
 "   15. Laertias Philenor; chrysalis, side view.
 "   16. Euphœades Glaucus.
 "   17. Laertias Philenor; chrysalis, dorsal view.

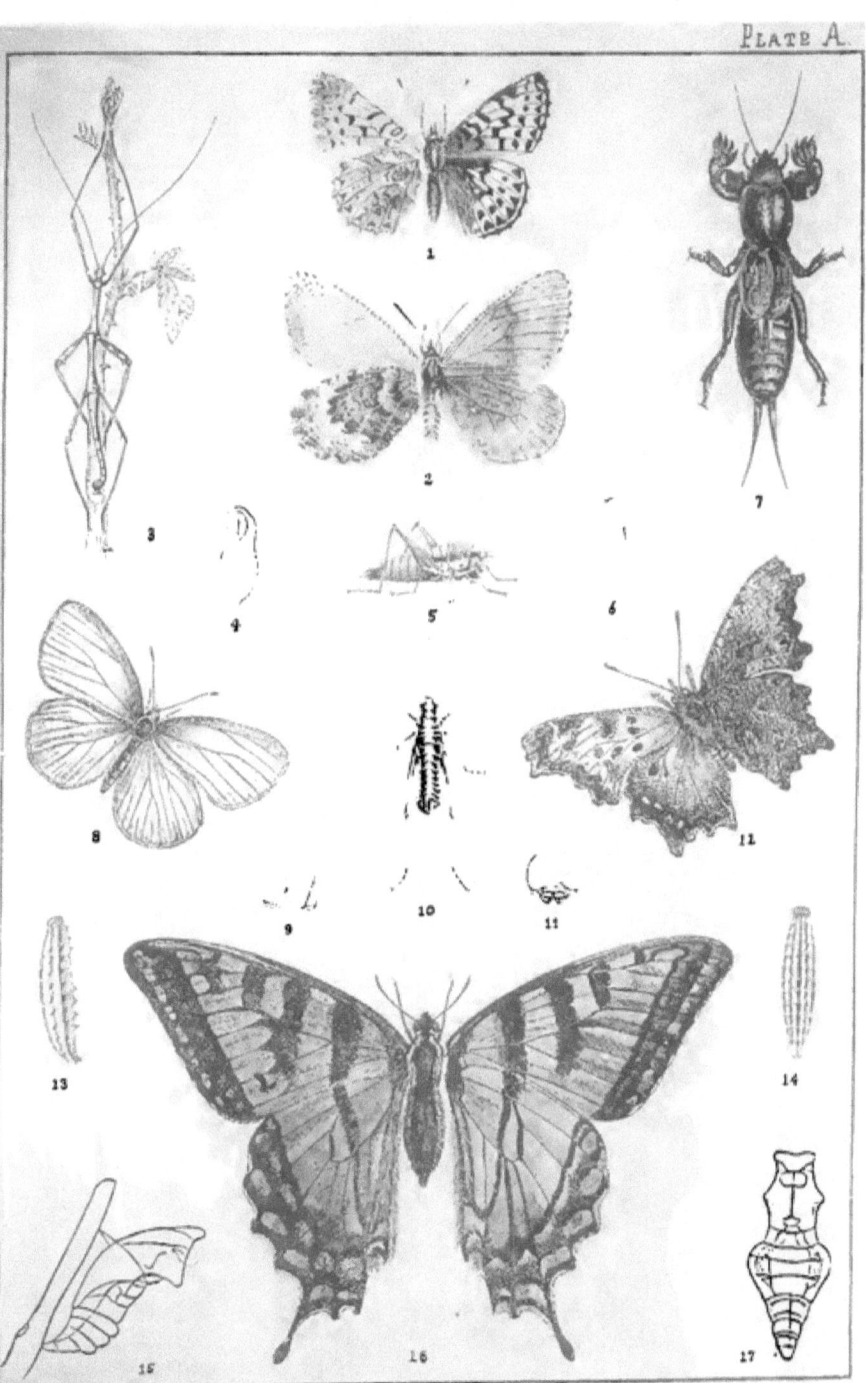

New Hampshire Insects.

INDEX TO CHAPTER XII.